THE
NEW SOUTHERN
TABLE

© 2014 Fair Winds Press
Text © 2014 Brys Stephens

First published in the USA in 2014 by
Fair Winds Press, a member of
Quayside Publishing Group
100 Cummings Center
Suite 406-L
Beverly, MA 01915-6101
www.fairwindspress.com
Visit www.QuarrySPOON.com and help us celebrate food and
culture one spoonful at a time!

17 16 15 14 13   1 2 3 4 5
ISBN: 978-1-59233-585-5
Digital edition published in 2013
eISBN: 978-62788-012-1

Library of Congress Cataloging-in-Publication Data available

Cover and Book design by Kathie Alexander
Photography by Brys Stephens

Printed and bound in China

The information in this book is for educational purposes only. It is not intended to replace the advice of a physician or medical practitioner. Please see your health care provider before beginning any new health program.

THE
NEW SOUTHERN

❧ CLASSIC INGREDIENTS REVISITED ❧

TABLE

BRYS STEPHENS

Fair Winds Press
100 Cummings Center, Suite 406L
Beverly, MA 01915

fairwindspress.com • quarryspoon.com

❧ CONTENTS ❧

My great-great-great-grandfather on my mother's side, a surgeon named David Ewart, studied medicine in Charleston, South Carolina, crossed the Atlantic to study in Paris, then returned to Charleston to serve as a surgeon in the Civil War.

David Ewart's great-grandson, Charles Whitten Walter, was born in Birmingham, Alabama. "C. Witty," as his friends called him, was my grandfather, and I came by my love of gardening and cooking from him and my mother. He grew vegetables such as Jerusalem artichokes, cucumbers, and cabbage, and he pickled them in ceramic crocks. Memories of visiting his house are infused with the aroma of freshly baked biscuits, hickory smoke wafting from a smoker filled with pork shoulder, slabs of ribs and whole chickens, and the pungent, vinegary mop sauce that kept them moist.

My paternal grandfather, a third-generation Alabamian, grew up on a farm in southeastern Alabama. Even after settling in Birmingham, he maintained a deep love for the Southern crops he knew from his youth and held on to pecan groves and acres of high-bush blueberries near his hometown in Barbour County. Before dinners at his house in Birmingham, I'd walk into the kitchen and watch African-American cooks dressed in white tend to flour-scattered cutting boards, hot ovens, and cast-iron pots of "grease." One of the cooks, Mamie, sat on a stool tending to a deep fryer, using her thumb and forefinger

to roll spoonfuls of cornmeal batter into the hot oil. She called it hot water corn bread and showed me how to bob and turn the dumplings around with a slotted spoon until they were set and golden, then drain them on a brown paper bag. Susie, another cook, tended to splattering fried chicken at the stove.

When dinner was ready, the cooks would pass platters of food from the kitchen through a folding partition over the counter to the dining room: mottle-crusted buttermilk fried chicken, steamy plain white rice with gravy, fresh-shucked corn on the cob slathered in butter, vinegary stewed collard greens, sweet potato casserole, field peas, fried okra, corn bread, fresh rolls, chocolate pie, sweet rolls, and coffee. Those traditional Southern meals were a blend of soul and country, a legacy of slavery and settlement, and they imbued me with a feel for the fundamental roots of Southern cooking.

When I was thirteen, my family spent the summer in a house we rented in the South of France, near Nice. I remember our first jet-lagged breakfast in France: We had fresh-baked croissants made that morning and delivered to a breadbox attached to the mailbox. We spread them with room-temperature butter and preserves made from Provençal apricots and ate them on the patio overlooking herb-covered hillsides and the sea below. The Mediterranean sun was brighter than the tropical grey Birmingham summer. The air was dry and brisk, fragrant with the sea and herbs, and I had never tasted anything so sweet, buttery, and delicate in my life.

As we traveled all over Provence, I saw fresh rabbits, game birds, and cured sausages hanging from the rafters of the butcher shops. Fromagiers offered eggs and potent, farmy cheeses, and bakers displayed fragrant fresh-baked baguettes and pastries. At outdoor stalls, we found seasonal fruits, vegetables, and olives. We had hours-long lunches during the heat of the day. Everything looked, smelled, and tasted more alive—shockingly so at the time—than the ingredients from the Winn-Dixie at home.

While it wasn't until years later that I realized how much that summer taught me about the way that geography and climate influence the flavor of food, that first trip to France sparked a curiosity about everything farm, food, and plate. France made me want to see the world and break away from the Southern culinary tradition I knew from Birmingham, a tradition that had always seemed comforting but now seemed stifling.

That wanderlust drew me back to Europe after college. I moved to Paris, where beautiful food was everywhere. Many of the best-known Parisian bistros and brasseries specialized in cuisines from different regions of France, and I absorbed those regional ingredient combinations into my culinary repertoire. At l'Ami Louis, huge spring asparagus and green peas the size of marbles were paired with butter and fresh mint. Brasserie Bofinger served platters of choucroute garnie and Pinot Blanc from Alsace. At Au Trou Gascon, they served cassoulet with duck,

sausages, and white beans from the southwest France. There were delicate steamed fish, boiled potatoes with butter, and cream-based sauces with herbs from Brittany and Normandy. I wandered the daily outdoor markets, explored the countryside vineyards and farms, and cooked my way through Patricia Wells's Bistro Cooking, Anne Willan's French Regional Cooking, Richard Olney's Simple French Food, and Mireille Johnston's The Cuisine of the Sun.

After Paris and a stint at Chris Hastings's Hot and Hot Fish Club in Birmingham, I moved to Rome, where I rented a small apartment a few blocks from the Campo dei Fiori market. I picked up Italian and wandered the city for hours on end, there to study but inspired by the food. Market stalls overflowed with summer squash along with their blossoms, artichokes still attached to long thick stalks, and bright celestial heads of broccoli and cauliflower. My neighborhood shops sold crusty oven-fired pizzas and breads that sold out by noon each day, fresh pastas, unbelievably good cured meats and cheeses, and chalky-green olive oils. With books by Elizabeth David and Marcella Hazan in hand, I cooked and ate from those markets and shops. More than anything, I learned firsthand to respect the old adage that what grows together goes together. Taste and flavor were functions of time and place.

After I left Rome and traveled, I was imprinted with still more culinary and geographical associations. Markets in Sicily, with their Greek and Arab influences, were in many ways more similar to the markets I'd see later in Morocco and Egypt than those in Italy. The boisterous vendors with their harsh staccato accents sold olives, citrus, spices, and meats and cheeses from goats and lamb.

In Spain, markets and restaurants in Madrid offered cow's milk cheeses and comforting cooking like I'd find back in Paris. Down south in Andalucia, with its ancient Moorish influence, the arid landscape was covered with olive and orange trees. Morocco was a little bit like southern Spain, but even more like the Middle East, with its Berber traditions, and fruits and spices I'd never encountered. From Egypt and the Mediterranean to Jordan and the Red Sea, the cuisine became even less familiar. In Israel, foods were a mix of the Middle East and the Mediterranean, with hummus and eggplant, za'tar and olive oil. These culinary patterns inspired by landscape had evolved over eons, and I would look back to them in my own Southern cooking.

Once I finally moved back to the South—to Charleston—I began reviewing local restaurants and found work writing, consulting, and testing cookbooks. By now, chefs, farmers, writers, and artisans were exploring and reviving the South's culinary traditions from the roots up. Just in Charleston alone, Sean Brock was digging up and digging into the history of the South's heirloom seeds, grains, vegetables, and heritage meats. Mike Lata, who had spent time cooking in Provence, was celebrating the Lowcountry's local seafood. Many other chefs and cooks in Charleston were rediscovering the agricultural and culinary history of the Lowcountry, which began in the kitchens of the Carolina rice plantations, with their European, African, and Caribbean influences.

I began exploring the Caribbean, Central America, and South America, where many of the quintessentially Southern ingredients I knew from home also had roots. In Peru, lima beans were everywhere, and sweet potatoes and corn were served alongside Japanese- and Spanish-inspired ceviches. I traveled to Japan and Southeast Asia, where I saw even more of those "Southern" ingredients than I had seen in Italy, France, and Spain. Okra, watermelon, corn, sweet potatoes, and lima beans were abundant in Vietnamese and Thai markets, and I felt my culinary life coming full circle at the same time that Southern cooking was. I came to see that Southern cooking itself was a complex, multivarious thing, much more expansive than I'd ever imagined it to be over those soul-and-country meals I ate growing up.

This cookbook grew from the understanding of the essentially hopeful idea that Southern food today, despite its longstanding reputation as "y'all" cuisine, can, like the best cooking everywhere, be fueled by the quality of local ingredients. So why not look both to Southern tradition and to those many cuisines around the world that have developed age-old flavor combinations, techniques, and dishes based on the very same "Southern" ingredients I find in markets right here at home? That, to me, is what the New Southern Table is about.

OKRA

Like the South itself, okra is quirky and misunderstood. Brought here from its native Africa on slave ships, okra is thoroughly at home in the intense heat, inconsistent rainfall, and humidity of the South.

As a kid in Alabama, I remember driving down to my family's beach house on the Gulf Coast. On a steamy, grey summer day, we descended from the hills of Birmingham through the rolling peach farms of Chilton County, then down through the rich soil of the Black Belt near Montgomery. Cotton, corn, and soybeans covered the fields along the rural roads. We stopped at local farm stands, hopped out of the car into oppressive heat and humidity, and bought fresh okra by the bagful. Okra echoed that climate, which was both familiar and forbidding.

When we finally got down to the gulf, we went out fishing in the early morning and caught red snapper and grouper. On the way back from town, we bought pristine local white shrimp and Apalachicola oysters. Back at the house, we made gumbo with fresh tomatoes and fish stock, then added in that thinly sliced South Alabama okra a few minutes before the gumbo was done. The bright green okra gave the gumbo body, crunchy texture, and a bold vegetable flavor to the broth.

I grow okra every summer in my garden out on Sullivan's Island. As the plant grows, the okra pods develop along the plant's mature main stem, the ends pointing and curling upward. The plant's elegant yellow flowers with chocolate centers burst open and perfume the developing pods. There's nothing like picking pristine baby okra pods and simply cooking them on the same day. Warm from the sun, their soft fuzzy exterior gives off an orange like floral aroma.

In part because of its lurking interior sliminess, okra can be intimidating to home cooks. But it's an incredibly versatile vegetable, and it's easy to prepare. Grown in temperate and tropical climates the world over—from the Mediterranean and India to Southeast Asia and Japan—okra has an endearingly delicate flavor brought out when steamed until just barely bright green, then tossed with butter, quickly roasted at high heat with just a little olive oil and sea salt, or boiled and drizzled with shoyu and horseradish.

I also like to match okra with bold flavors: Indian-spiced okra with cumin, and coriander and mustard seeds; a Vietnamese sweet-and-sour fish soup; a Greek-inspired pairing of okra, tomato, and feta. No matter what, I almost always cook okra until just done and bright green or a tad beyond, which is good for getting the most from its flavor and texture. Cook it too long and it'll be too soft. Whether treated gently with steam to coax out its delicate flavors, or manhandled with high heat and assertive flavors, okra is a worldly addition to the Southern table.

❧ Roasted Okra with Olive Oil, Lemon, and Sea Salt ❧

This is one of the simplest ways I know to cook okra. The high heat from the oven concentrates the okra's flavor, and the olive oil, lemon, and sea salt are the minimal seasoning that the okra flavor needs.

2 pounds (905 g) okra, any tough stem ends trimmed away and discarded

3 tablespoons (45 ml) olive oil

Sea salt

Lemon wedges

Preheat the oven to 450°F (230°C, or gas mark 8). In a bowl, toss the okra with the olive oil to coat. Arrange the okra in a single layer on a large sheet pan. Roast 8 to 10 minutes, or until bright green, barely tender, and brown in spots. Serve immediately with the sea salt and lemon wedges.

YIELD: **4** TO **6** SERVINGS

৶ Grilled Okra with Smoked Paprika and Mint Yogurt ৶

Like other dry heat cooking methods, grilling concentrates okra's flavor and gives it great texture. Here, the paprika in the yogurt sauce complements and brings out the smokiness imparted by the grill. I like to use full-fat Greek yogurt for its richness.

2 cups (460 g) Greek yogurt

1 tablespoon (15 ml) fresh lemon juice

1 teaspoon (2 g) lemon zest

2 teaspoons (5 g) smoked paprika

2 tablespoons (12 g) minced fresh mint

2 to 4 tablespoons (28 to 60 ml) water

Kosher salt and cayenne pepper

2 pounds (905 g) okra, any tough ends trimmed away and discarded

Olive oil

In a medium-size bowl, whisk together the yogurt, lemon juice, lemon zest, paprika, and mint. Whisk in just enough water so that the yogurt has a pourable sauce consistency. Season to taste with salt and cayenne pepper.

Preheat the grill to high. Brush the okra with olive oil, and season lightly with salt. When the grill is very hot, grill the okra, turning once, 4 to 6 minutes, or until charred and tender. To serve, drizzle the okra with the yogurt.

YIELD: **4** TO **6** SERVINGS

❧ Japanese-Style Okra with Horseradish Soy Dressing ❧

The simplicity of this traditional Japanese cooking method—gently boiling the okra in lightly salted water until just done—highlights the okra's flavor. The simple shoyu-based sauce is flavorful and salty with a little nasal heat from the horseradish.

Cook the okra in lightly salted boiling water 2 to 4 minutes, or until bright green and barely tender. Drain in a colander, rinse with cold water until cooled, and pat dry with a kitchen towel.

Place the mirin in a small saucepan, bring to a gentle simmer, then remove from the heat. This will cook off the alcohol. Let cool slightly. When cool, combine the mirin, soy sauce, and horseradish in a medium-size bowl.

Serve the okra at room temperature or chilled, drizzled with the dressing.

YIELD: **4** TO **6** SERVINGS

2 pounds okra (905 g), any tough ends trimmed away and discarded

Kosher salt

¼ cup (60 ml) mirin

¼ cup (235 ml) soy sauce, preferably Japanese shoyu

1 tablespoon (15 g) prepared horseradish, finely grated fresh horseradish (8 g), or fresh wasabi (10 g)

ᘓ **Greek-Style Okra with Tomato, Feta, and Marjoram** ᘒ

Okra and tomatoes is a classic Southern combination. Here, greek-inspired additions of feta and fresh marjoram add silky texture and woodsy aroma to the okra, and a touch of heat from the red pepper flakes add even more flavor.

Place the okra in a large glass or plastic bowl, toss with the vinegar to coat, and season with the 1 tablespoon (18 g) of the salt. Toss to combine, and set aside for at least 20 minutes and up to 1 hour, stirring once or twice; rinse the okra well in a colander, and pat dry.

Heat the olive oil in a large heavy skillet over medium heat. Add the shallot and red pepper flakes and cook, stirring frequently, 2 to 3 minutes. Add the tomato paste and cook, stirring frequently, to toast it on the bottom of the pan, 1 to 2 minutes.

Add the okra, tomatoes, the ¼ teaspoon (1.5 g) salt, and 1 cup (235 ml) water, bring to a boil, cover, and cook, stirring occasionally, about 20 minutes, or until the sauce thickens and the okra is tender. Add a little water if the pan gets dry as the okra cooks. Add the marjoram and feta, stir to combine, and season to taste with salt and pepper.

YIELD: **4** TO **6** SERVINGS

2 pounds (905 g) okra, any tough stem ends trimmed away and discarded

¼ cup (60 ml) red wine vinegar

1 tablespoon and ¼ teaspoon (19.5 g) kosher salt, divided, plus more to taste

2 tablespoons (28 ml) olive oil

1 medium-size shallot, diced

½ teaspoon red pepper flakes

2 tablespoons (32 g) tomato paste

2 medium-size tomatoes, chopped, or 2 cups (500 g) tomato purée

1 cup (235 ml) water, plus more as needed

2 teaspoons (1.2 g) minced fresh marjoram

4 ounces (115 g) feta cheese, crumbled

Freshly ground black pepper

❧ Indian-Spiced Okra with Chickpeas ❧

Okra is common throughout Asia, especially in India, where it's called *lady fingers*. Its earthy flavor benefits from an array of bold Indian spices. The deeply toasted tomato paste adds depth of flavor; and the chickpeas are a healthy addition that also adds texture. This dish works as a side or as a main course over any grain.

3 tablespoons (45 ml) vegetable oil

2 tablespoons (22 g) mustard seeds

1 tablespoon (6 g) cumin seeds

4 cloves garlic, thinly sliced

1½ pounds (680 g) okra, any tough stem ends trimmed off and discarded

3 tablespoons (48 g) tomato paste

1½ cups (360 g) chickpeas, rinsed and drained (1 can, 15 ounces, or 430 g)

1 cup (235 ml) water, or less as needed

Kosher salt

Freshly ground black pepper

Heat the oil in a large, heavy skillet over medium heat. Add the mustard seeds and cumin seeds, and cover as the mustard seeds will start to pop. Shake the pan 1 to 2 minutes, or until the popping subsides. Add the garlic and cook 30 seconds. Add the okra and cook, stirring for 1 minute. Add the tomato paste (which may splatter, so be careful) and stir to coat the okra and to toast the tomato paste on the bottom of the pan, 1 to 2 minutes. Add the chickpeas and enough water to coat the bottom of the pan; season lightly with salt and pepper, and cover. Cook, stirring occasionally, 3 to 5 minutes, or until the okra is bright green. Uncover the skillet and cook, stirring frequently, another 2 to 4 minutes, or until the sauce thickens and the okra is tender. Season to taste with salt and pepper.

YIELD: **4** TO **6** SERVINGS

❧ Okra, Andouille, and Quinoa Pilau ❧

Pilaus (or pilafs, or *perloos*) have deep Southern and especially Lowcountry roots, and made their way here with French Huguenot planters from the South of France. This is a straight-forward Southern-inspired pilau, except that it's made with quinoa, not rice, which gives it a unique texture and a protein punch.

Bring 3 cups (710 ml) of water to a bare simmer in a medium saucepan.

Heat the olive oil in a large, heavy, high-sided skillet over medium-high heat. Squeeze the sausage out of the casings, form it into small semiround pieces, and drop them into the oil. Cook, stirring occasionally, about 2 minutes, or until lightly browned. Add the onion and cook, stirring frequently, another 2 to 4 minutes, or until the onion is translucent. Add the thyme leaves and drained quinoa and cook, stirring frequently, 2 to 4 minutes, or until the quinoa is dry and lightly toasted. Add the tomato purée, and cook 1 to 3 minutes, or until much of the purée has reduced and darkened in color. Add the okra, simmering water, and golden raisins, and stir to combine. Bring to a boil, reduce to a simmer, and cook, uncovered, 10 to 15 minutes, or until the quinoa is tender and most of the liquid has evaporated. Cover, and set aside for 10 minutes before serving. Season to taste with salt and pepper.

YIELD: **6 TO 8 SERVINGS**

3 cups (710 ml) water

2 tablespoons (28 ml) olive oil

2 fresh andouille sausages

1 yellow onion, diced

1 teaspoon (2.4 g) fresh thyme leaves, chopped

2 cups (346 g) quinoa, rinsed and drained well

1 cup (250 g) tomato purée

3/4 pound (340 g) okra, tough part of ends trimmed off and discarded, cut into 1/4-inch (13 mm) rounds

1/2 cup (75 g) golden raisins

1/2 teaspoon kosher salt, plus more to taste

Black pepper

⚙ Also known as a *pilaf*, *perloo*, and *peleau*, a *pilau* is a rice-and-broth-based dish that includes any combination of aromatic vegetables, beans, meats, and spices. Pilafs probably originated in Persia, and then spread all over the world, including Southern France, where it was adopted by French Huguenots who would later settle the South Carolina Lowcountry.

✂ Hot, Sweet, and Sour Fish Soup ✂

On a trip to Vietnam last year, I took a boat ride in the Mekong Delta with a guide, and we had a bowl of this soup in a tiny restaurant run by a small family. This soup exemplifies everything I love about Vietnamese cooking. The broth is nourishing, and the balance of sweet (from the pineapple) and sour (from the tamarind) makes you want more with every bite.

Combine the tamarind pulp and water in a large saucepan, and bring to a boil, pressing the pulp to break it apart. Reduce the heat and simmer for 5 minutes. Strain through a fine-mesh sieve, reserving liquid, pressing the pulp until all the liquid is removed. Discard the pulp and return the tamarind broth to a simmer.

Heat the oil in a medium-size, heavy stockpot over medium-high heat. Add the shallot, chile, lemongrass, and star anise, and cook, stirring often, 4 to 6 minutes, or until the shallot is translucent. Add the simmering tamarind broth, fish sauce, and sugar, and bring to a boil. Reduce the heat, and simmer 6 to 8 minutes. Immediately remove the star anise. Season to taste with salt.

Add the fish, pineapple, and okra, and gently simmer 4 to 6 minutes, or until fish is cooked through and the okra is bright green and tender. Add the tomato and sprouts, and remove the saucepan from the heat. Add more fish sauce and sugar, to taste. Discard the lemongrass. Serve with the cilantro and lime wedges.

YIELD: **4** TO **6** SERVINGS

4 ounces (115 g) seedless tamarind pulp, sliced into pieces

6 cups (1.4 L) water

1 tablespoon (15 ml) vegetable oil

1 large shallot, thinly sliced

1 Thai or jalapeño chile, thinly sliced

1 stalk lemongrass, cut into a 4-inch (10 cm) length, outer layers peeled away, and lightly pounded with the back of a knife

1 small star anise

½ cup (120 ml) fish sauce

1 tablespoon (15 g) palm sugar or light brown sugar

Kosher salt

1 pound (455 g) catfish, flounder, or any white-fleshed fish, cut into 1-inch (25 mm) pieces

1 cup (165 g) cubed fresh pineapple

½ pound (225 g) okra, the smaller the better, tough part of stems trimmed and discarded, cut into 1-inch (25 mm) lengths (or left whole if small)

1 ripe tomato, cut into 1-inch (2.5 cm) pieces

2 cups (100 g) mung bean sprouts

Fresh cilantro leaves

Lime wedges

⚙ *Com chua*, meaning "sour soup" in Vietnamese, is a soup that originated in Vietnam's Mekong Delta and is made with tamarind, pineapple, and tomatoes. It can also include vegetables such as okra, herbs such as basil or cilantro, and either fish (*com chua ca*), shrimp (*canh chua tom*), or chicken (*canh chua ga*).

Panhandle Seafood Gumbo

This gumbo, especially when packed with okra, oysters, shrimp, and red snapper, transports me back to our house in Seagrove Beach on the Florida Panhandle. Don't rush the roux; patience will yield a gumbo with beautiful color and rich flavor.

- ½ cup (120 ml) vegetable oil
- ½ cup (63 g) all-purpose flour
- 1 medium onion, diced
- Kosher salt and freshly ground black pepper
- 1 stalk celery, diced
- 1 green bell pepper, diced
- 1 red bell pepper, diced
- 3 cloves garlic, minced
- 3 tablespoons (48 g) tomato paste
- 1 teaspoon (1 g) fresh thyme leaves
- 10 cups (2.4 L) chicken stock, simmering
- 3 tablespoons (45 ml) Worcestershire sauce
- 2 bay leaves
- 4 smoked andouille sausages, sliced
- 2 cups (200 g) thick-sliced okra rounds
- 1 pound (455 g) fresh shrimp, peeled and deveined
- 1 pound (455 g) very fresh white-fleshed fish, cut into 1-inch (2.5 cm) pieces
- 1 cup (248 g) shucked oysters with their juice
- Cayenne pepper

Heat the oil in a large, heavy stockpot over medium-high heat. When the oil is hot, whisk in the flour, and stir to combine well. Reduce the heat to medium and cook, stirring often and adjusting the heat as necessary to prevent scorching, 15 to 20 minutes, or until the roux is deep brown.

Add the onion, season lightly with salt and black pepper, and cook, stirring often, 8 to 10 minutes, or until soft; reduce the heat as needed if the onions cook too quickly. Add the celery and bell peppers, and cook, stirring frequently, 4 to 6 minutes, or until the peppers start to turn soft. Add the tomato paste and cook, stirring, 1 minute. Add the garlic and thyme and cook until just fragrant, about 1 minute.

Add the chicken stock, Worcestershire sauce, bay leaves, and sausage to the stockpot, and simmer, partially covered, for 30 minutes, skimming the fat from the surface from time to time. Stir in the okra, and cook another 15 minutes.

Add the shrimp and fish, and gently simmer 2 to 4 minutes, or until the seafood is cooked through. Stir in the oysters and their liquid, turn off the heat, cover, and set the gumbo aside for 5 minutes, just long enough for the edges of the oysters to curl. Remove and discard the bay leaves. Season to taste with salt and cayenne pepper. Serve with rice.

SERVES 4 TO 6 SERVINGS

Gumbo is a soup or stew that originated in Louisiana in the 1700s. It's made with Louisiana's holy trinity of aromatics—celery, bell peppers, and onions—plus broth, thickened with either okra or filé powder, and may include shellfish and other seafood, chicken, sausage, and game. Gumbo likely got its name from a West African word for okra, *ki ngombo.*

FIELD PEAS

When I was growing up, field peas were one of the celebrated gifts of summer. Shelled and bagged at a fresh farm market called Murphree's, a mile or so from our house in Birmingham, fresh field peas would show up all summer, and we'd freeze them to have on hand throughout the year.

Each summer in Charleston, I horde every kind of field pea I can find, whether dried or fresh, including sea island red peas, an heirloom variety of field pea that got its name from the nearby sea islands where they grew. They have a beautiful reddish color and are thought to be the principal bean incorporated into the classic Lowcountry Hoppin' John, a version of which I include here.

Field peas, also known as southern peas or cowpeas, are a legume likely native to Africa, and a different genus than both lima beans (or butter beans) and common beans (such as red beans and black beans), which are native to the Americas. There are countless varieties of field peas—black-eyed peas, purple hull peas, pink-eye peas, lady peas, cream peas, and crowder peas—and most of them came to the Americas with ships of the slave trade.

Fresh or frozen field peas cook quickly in boiling salted water, only about 15 or 20 minutes depending on when they were picked. One of the most pleasurable ways to eat field peas is one of the simplest: warmed through with olive oil or butter, seasoned with salt and freshly ground black pepper, piled on top of a mound of rice or quinoa, with hot pepper vinegar or hot sauce.

Dried field peas, on the other hand, should be soaked overnight, rinsed and drained, then brought to a boil. I cook them just like I do dried beans, flavored with whatever I have on hand: some member of the onion family (onion, leek, shallot), something with a little heat (fresh or dried chiles, peppercorns), a few sprigs of fresh herbs (parsley, thyme, sage, marjoram), and sometimes something meaty such as a smoked turkey wing, ham hock, or piece of bacon. The broth they make is delicious by itself, and can be eaten as a soup.

I also like to use them in unusual ways, and look to other cuisines that cook with beans and legumes for inspiration. I incorporate field peas into a flavorful Mediterranean tabouleh salad, toss them with pasta and fresh summer pesto the way the Italians would white beans, and simmer them in an intensely flavored curry, with pork, as they would in South Asia.

Despite its traveling history, the humble field pea is in a way a secret of the South and a versatile poor man's food rich in both history and flavor.

❧ Coconut Hoppin' John ❧

This tropically inspired version of the classic Hoppin' John of the South Carolina Lowcountry was probably originally made with local varieties of field peas. Any kind of broth would do here, but the combination of coconut, tomato, and the bacon-infused peas is what makes this version of a humble dish a little less so.

In a large bowl, cover the peas generously with water, soak overnight, then drain, and rinse well.

Heat the oil in a large, heavy stockpot over medium heat. Add the bacon and cook about 5 minutes, or until the bacon has browned and the fat has rendered. Add the shallot, 1 teaspoon (6 g) salt, the pepper, red pepper flakes, and thyme, and cook, stirring often, another 5 minutes, or until the shallot is tender.

Add the coconut milk, tomato purée, chicken stock, and bay leaf, and bring to a boil. Reduce the heat and simmer for 10 minutes. Stir in the peas, and simmer, uncovered, at a gentle boil for 20 to 30 minutes, or until the peas are tender but still have some resistance.

Stir in the rice and cook, uncovered, stirring ocasionally to prevent sticking, another 20 to 30 minutes, until much of the liquid is absorbed. Remove from the heat and set aside, covered, for 10 minutes before serving. Remove and discard the bay leaf. Season to taste with salt and pepper.

YIELD: **6 SERVINGS**

1 cup (165 g) sea island red peas

2 teaspoons (10 ml) vegetable oil

3 slices thick-cut bacon, diced

2 medium-size shallots, diced

1 teaspoon (6 g) kosher salt, plus more to taste

1/2 teaspoon freshly ground black pepper, plus more to taste

1/2 teaspoon red pepper flakes

1 teaspoon (1.5 g) chopped fresh thyme

1 can (13 to 14 ounces, or 395 to 425 ml) light coconut milk (about 1 1/2 cups)

1 1/4 cups (295 ml) tomato purée

4 1/2 cups (355 ml) chicken stock or water

1 bay leaf

1 1/2 cups (278 g) long-grain rice, preferably basmati, rinsed with cold water until the water runs clear

🥄 Hoppin' John is a classic Southern rice and bean dish that originated in the South Carolina and Georgia Lowcountry. It's a humble dish of rice and field peas that likely originally included the Carolina Gold variety of rice, and the sea island variety of red peas. Hoppin' may be a corruption of the French Creole term for black-eyed peas, *pois pigeons.*

❧ Pork and Field Pea Curry ❧

This is a (relatively) simplified version of a flavorful South Asian curry, perfumed with ginger, shallot, fresh turmeric, and spices. Field peas aren't traditional in South Asian curries, though curry powder was a surprisingly common ingredient in the South in Colonial times. The field peas stand up to the pork, mushrooms, and bold curry flavors beautifully here, much like lentils and chickpeas would in traditional curries.

Place the cumin seeds, coriander seeds, cardamom pods, cloves, mustard seeds, and peppercorns in a dry skillet over medium heat and toast, stirring often, 3 to 5 minutes, or until fragrant. Grind in a spice grinder or mortar and pestle, or put the spices in a resealable plastic bag and crush them with a heavy skillet until ground. Transfer the ground spices to a bowl, and stir in the habañero chile powder, ½ teaspoon salt, and cinnamon.

Using a food processor or mortar and pestle, combine the turmeric, ginger, shallot, and garlic, and purée or pound until very smooth.

Heat the ¼ cup (60 ml) of coconut cream in a medium-size saucepan over medium heat. Add the spice mixture and cook, stirring often, 2 minutes. Add the ground ginger and shallot mixture and cook, stirring often, 6 to 8 minutes, or until toasted and reduced. Adjust the heat as necessary so the spices don't scorch.

Stir in the remaining coconut milk and the chicken stock, and bring to a boil. Reduce to a simmer and cook 5 minutes. Add the carrots, the white part of the spring onions, field peas, mushrooms, and pork, and cook, stirring often, 6 to 8 minutes, or until the pork is just cooked through. Stir in the green part of the scallions, the lime zest, and basil, and season to taste with salt.

YIELD: 4 TO 6 SERVINGS

4 teaspoons (9.5 g) cumin seeds

4 teaspoons (7 g) coriander seeds

8 cardamom pods

4 whole cloves

1 teaspoon (4 g) mustard seeds

1 teaspoon (2 g) black peppercorns

⅛ teaspoon habañero chile powder or cayenne pepper

½ teaspoon kosher salt, plus more to taste

½ teaspoon ground cinnamon

2 pieces fresh turmeric, 2-inches (5 cm) long each, peeled and sliced, or 1 teaspoon (2 g) ground turmeric

1 piece ginger, 4 inches (10 cm) long, peeled and sliced

2 medium-size shallots, peeled and sliced

2 cloves garlic, peeled

3 cups (710 ml) coconut milk, with ¼ cup (60 ml) cream skimmed from the top of the can

1½ cups (355 ml) chicken stock

2 medium-size carrots, thinly sliced

2 medium-size scallions, thinly sliced, white and green parts separated

3½ cups (595 g) cooked field peas

6 medium-size shiitake mushrooms, stemmed and thinly sliced

1 pound (455 g) pork loin, thinly sliced

1 teaspoon (2 g) lime zest

6 to 8 basil leaves, torn

🫛 *Curry* is a generic English term that refers to any dish containing either curry powder, or a diverse array of fresh ingredients that add up to curry flavor, such as spices, fresh or dried chiles, and coconut milk. Curries can be wet or dry, and can include any combination of meat or vegetables. Curries originated in South and Southeast Asia, and spread all over the world with the British colonial empire as early as the 1700s.

⸙ Beet, Field Pea, Radish, and Arugula Salad ⸙

When the cooler weather comes to Charleston, I like to make salads with colorful watermelon radishes, beets, and arugula as they come into season. The field peas, which I keep dried or frozen, add great texture.

Preheat the oven to 350°F (180°C, or gas mark 4). Place the beets directly on the oven rack, and roast 45 to 60 minutes, or until a paring knife inserted into the centers of the beets easily pierces them. Transfer the beets to a plate until cool enough to handle, then peel and thinly slice them. Arrange the beets and radishes in an overlapping pattern on each plate. In a bowl, combine the field peas, arugula, cheese, dill, olive oil, lemon juice, and season to taste with salt and pepper; gently toss to combine. Mound this mixture in the center of each plate, and drizzle the beets and radishes with additional olive oil and lemon juice.

YIELD: **4 SERVINGS**

4 medium beets, scrubbed

½ pound (225 g) watermelon radishes or other radishes, thinly sliced

2 cups (340 g) cooked field peas

4 ounces (115 g) arugula

4 ounces (115 g) ricotta salata or other firm, salty cheese

1 tablespoon (4 g) chopped fresh dill

3 tablespoons (45 ml) olive oil, plus more to taste

2 tablespoons (28 ml) lemon juice, plus more to taste

Kosher salt and freshly ground black pepper

❧ **Purple Hull Pea Tabouleh** ❧

Tabouleh, a classic Middle Eastern salad boldly flavored with parsley, goes well with field peas. Matched with the bulgur and the tart lemony dressing, the peas make this salad a protein-filled and refreshing meal in itself.

Bring the water to a boil in a large saucepan, stir in the bulgur and the ½ teaspoon salt, and simmer gently, 10 to 15 minutes, or until the bulgur is tender. Drain, rinse the bulgur with cold water, and set aside until completely drained, stirring occasionally to help this process along.

In a large bowl, combine the drained bulgur, field peas, cucumber, tomatoes, parsley, mint, lemon juice, and olive oil, and season to taste with salt, black pepper, and red pepper flakes. Chill the salad for at least two hours for best flavor.

YIELD: **6** TO **8** SERVINGS

4 cups (945 ml) water

1 cup (225 g) bulgur

½ teaspoon kosher salt, plus more to taste

4 cups (680 g) cooked field peas

2 cups (270 g) diced cucumber

2 cups (360 g) diced tomatoes

2 cups (120 g) chopped fresh parsley

¼ cup (100 g) chopped fresh mint

½ cup (120 ml) fresh lemon juice

¾ cup (175 ml) olive oil

Freshly ground black pepper

Red pepper flakes

🖎 Tabouleh is a vegetable and grain salad of Levantine Arab origin, made with bulgur or couscous, tomatoes, cucumbers, and finely chopped parsley or mint, along with olive oil and lemon juice. It is one of the most popular Middle Eastern/Mediterranean dishes in the West.

❧ Tomato Salad with Crispy Okra and Field Pea Vinaigrette ❧

This elegant, comforting summer salad is all about the simplicity of the fresh summer tomatoes and field peas matched with the silky texture and tang of buttermilk. Crispy okra adds nice crunch.

To make the okra: Fill a large, heavy skillet with the oil to a depth of 1 inch (25 mm), and heat to 350°F (180°C). Whisk together the kosher salt, pepper, flour, and cornmeal in a large bowl, add the okra, and toss to combine. Remove the okra and place it in a fine-mesh strainer, and shake to remove any excess flour mixture. Place the buttermilk in a large bowl. Dip the okra one pod at a time into the buttermilk, then dredge again in the flour mixture, and shake off the excess. Carefully place each okra into the hot oil, and fry, turning once, 2 to 4 minutes per side, or until golden brown and crispy. Drain on a paper-towel-lined plate, and keep warm in an oven on low heat.

To make the vinaigrette: Whisk together the buttermilk, cider vinegar, and sugar in a medium bowl until well combined. Stir in the chives and field peas, and season to taste with salt, black pepper, and cayenne pepper.

To assemble the salad: Cut the tomatoes into thick slices, and divide them among each plate. Drizzle with the field pea vinaigrette, and top with the crispy okra.

YIELD: **4** SERVINGS

For the crispy okra:
Canola oil, for frying
1 teaspoon (6 g) kosher salt
1/2 teaspoon freshly ground black pepper
1/2 cup (60 g) all-purpose flour
1/4 cup (35 g) finely ground yellow cornmeal
10 okra pods
1/4 cup (60 ml) buttermilk

For the tomato salad and vinaigrette:
1/2 cup (60 ml) buttermilk
2 tablespoons (28 ml) cider vinegar
2 teaspoons (9 g) granulated sugar
2 tablespoons (6 g) minced fresh chives
1/2 cup (85 g) cooked field peas
Kosher salt
Freshly ground pepper
Cayenne pepper
4 medium-size ripe tomatoes

❧ Bowtie Pasta with Sea Island Red Peas and Pesto ❧

Italian and Southern cooking share a long history of making do with what you have, so the prevalence of starch and bean combinations in both cuisines is no surprise. Instead of white beans, which might be paired with pesto in Italy, I look to local sea island red peas. They're a great medium for the bold flavor of the pesto.

To make the pesto: Combine the basil leaves, garlic, and pine nuts in a food processor, and pulse two or three times until coarsely ground. Drizzle in the olive oil, and pulse until smooth. Scrape down the sides of the processor, add the Parmesan, and pulse until combined. Season to taste with salt and pepper.

To cook the pasta and peas: Cook the pasta in boiling salted water according to the package directions. Just before the pasta is al dente, add the field peas to the water with the pasta. Return to a boil, then drain the pasta and peas in a colander, reserving ½ cup (120 ml) of the pasta water.

To assemble: Transfer the pasta and field peas to a large bowl. Add the pesto to taste, a little at a time, and stir to incorporate. Add a little of the reserved pasta water if necessary to thin out the pesto. Garnish with the pine nuts, if desired .

YIELD: **4** TO **6** SERVINGS

For the pesto:

2½ cups (24 g) packed fresh basil leaves

1 clove garlic, peeled and coarsely chopped

⅓ cup (45 g) pine nuts

½ cup (120 ml) extra-virgin olive oil

1¼ cups (125 g) freshly grated Parmesan

Kosher salt and freshly ground black pepper

For the pasta:

1 pound (455 g) bowtie pasta

3 cups (510 g) cooked field peas

Optional garnish:

Pine nuts

᧙ **Black-Eyed Pea, Sausage, and Escarole Soup** ᧙

It's hard to go wrong with any combination of pork, greens, and beans, and this soup is no exception. I learned to cook escarole—a versatile, slightly bitter green, in Italy—where it's at home in soups, salads, and on the grill.

Heat the olive oil in a large, heavy stockpot over medium heat. Add the onion, salt, and red pepper flakes, and cook, stirring frequently, 2 to 4 minutes, or until the onion is translucent. While the onion is cooking, squeeze the sausage from the casing, forming it into small pieces. Add the small pieces of sausage to the onions. Cook 4 to 6 minutes, or until the sausage is brown. Add the rosemary and garlic, and cook 1 minute. Add the tomatoes and cook, stirring often, 4 to 6 minutes, or until the tomatoes darken in color. Add the chicken stock and water, and bring to a boil. Add the field peas and boil gently for 10 minutes. Add the escarole and lemon zest, and cook another 4 to 6 minutes, or until the escarole has wilted. Season to taste with salt and pepper. Garnish with grated pecorino cheese, if desired.

YIELD: **4** TO **6** SERVINGS

2 tablespoons (28 ml) olive oil

1 large onion, chopped

1 teaspoon (6 g) kosher salt, plus more to taste

½ teaspoon red pepper flakes

2 links sweet Italian sausage

1 teaspoon (1 g) minced fresh rosemary

2 cloves garlic, minced

½ cup (125 g) tomato purée or crushed tomatoes

3½ cups (830 ml) chicken stock

6 cups (1.4 L) water

3 cups (510 g) cooked field peas

1 pound (455 g) escarole, trimmed and chopped

1 teaspoon (2 g) grated lemon zest

Freshly ground black pepper

Optional garnish:

Pecorino cheese

❧ Flounder in Parchment with Field Peas, Squash, and Peppers ❧

I love cooking fish in parchment paper because the variations are endless and cleanup is easy. Just about any delicate white-fleshed fish is at home here with fresh vegetables from the garden. Any mix of fresh herbs works too, but delicate ones such as tarragon, chervil, and parsley are especially good with fish.

4 small yellow squash, thinly sliced

2 small red bell peppers, thinly sliced

4 large scallions, white and green parts, thinly sliced

4 teaspoons (7 g) grated lemon zest

3 tablespoons (12 g) coarsely chopped fresh delicate herbs (parsley, chervil, tarragon), plus more for garnish

1 teaspoon (1.2 g) dried red pepper flakes

3 teaspoons (18 g) kosher salt

3 tablespoons (45 ml) olive oil, plus more for drizzling

3 cups (510 g) cooked field peas

1/4 cup (60 ml) dry white wine

4 flounder fillets, 6 ounces (170 g) each

Optional garnishes:

Olive oil

Maldon or other coarse sea salt

Fresh herbs

Preheat the oven to 400°F (200°C, or gas mark 6).

Combine all the ingredients except the fish in a large bowl and toss to combine. Brush the flounder fillets with olive oil and season with a light sprinkling of salt on both sides.

Tear off eight sheets of parchment paper, 1-foot (30 cm) long each, from a roll. Lay four of the sheets out flat on a work surface, and divide one-half of the vegetable and herb mixture evenly among the four sheets, mounding it in the center of each sheet. Top each mound with a flounder filet, and top each flounder fillet with equal parts of the remaining vegetable and herb mixture.

Cover each sheet with one of the remaining sheets of parchment paper. To seal the parchment, fold over and crease the top and bottom sheets of paper together, working in a circle to close the parchment, making a sealed packet. If the packet won't stay sealed on its own, secure the folded end with a stapler.

Place the packets on sheet pans, and bake 15 to 20 minutes, or until the packets expand from the steam, and the fish is just cooked through. If you're in doubt, test one of the packets for doneness.

Place each packet on a plate, cut open and fold back the parchment paper, and garnish with more olive oil, Maldon salt, and fresh herbs, if desired.

YIELD: **4 SERVINGS**

SQUASH

As the recipes in this chapter show, I often look to simple cooking methods from Provence and Italy when cooking with summer squash. The buttery flavor of the squash goes well with olive oil, pancetta and prosciutto, chiles, and Italian cheeses such as pecorino and Parmesan. Like okra, squash is nicely balanced by acidic ingredients such as tomatoes, citrus, and vinegar.

When I lived near the Campo dei Fiori market in Rome, I'd wander over on market days at lunchtime and buy whatever looked good: a beautiful zucchini or two, some fresh oregano, a bagful of handmade cheese ravioli, and a wedge of Parmigiano-Reggiano. Back at my apartment, I'd boil the pasta, sauté the zucchini in a fruity, peppery olive oil, and toss it all together with a handful of grated Parmigiano-Reggiano and some red pepper flakes. It was a revelation of simplicity that I go back to over and over again.

Unfortunately, the reputation that zucchini and other summer squash have for being boring and bland is pretty well earned. Many of the zucchini and yellow squash available in grocery stores actually are bland, as they've been bred for durability and usually harvested after their flavor is best. Smaller, less common, and more interesting-looking varieties (especially straight from the garden or farmers' market) are much better.

To fully appreciate summer squash, you really need to experience kneeling down at a squash plant, moving the huge leaves out of the way, finding a squash 4 inches (10 cm) or so long with its blossom still attached, trimming it off with a knife, taking it into the kitchen, slicing it open to see droplets of water form on the freshly cut flesh, and cooking it right then.

Native to Mesoamerica, summer squash are also a natural fit with Mexican cooking. I love sautéed squash in tacos, quesadillas, and burritos. Summer squash are also incorporated into cuisines of the Mediterranean, from North Africa to the Middle East, and all the way across Asia. I love frying zucchini tempura-style like they do in Japan; the delicate batter and hot oil beautifully preserves the zucchini's moisture, and a simple soy-based sauce is the only other accompaniment they need. Summer squash are great in stir-fries, too, with beef, chicken, tofu, or pork.

Summer squash are different from the hard-fleshed or "winter" squash (butternut, acorn) that are more common in cooler climates. With softer skin and more tender flesh than the larger pumpkinlike varieties, summer squash are harvested in immature form. Varieties include green and golden zucchini; globe zucchini; yellow, straight-neck, and crooked-neck squash; patty pan squash; and the bi-color Zephyr. The volume and selection of squash overflowing in Charleston's farmers' markets every summer are something to see.

❧ Roman-Style Marinated Zucchini ❧

In Italian trattorias *alla scapece* is a common way of serving summer squash, peppers, and eggplant in the summer, set out on tables as antipasti. In this version, searing the zucchini before marinating it in vinegar, red pepper flakes, and mint makes for a simple dish with a complex array of flavors.

Generously sprinkle the zucchini slices on both sides with kosher salt to draw the excess moisture away from the zucchini. (This is more salt than you would normally season them with for eating. Some of the salt will penetrate, but some will be rinsed off.) Place the zucchini in a colander for 30 minutes, then rinse with cold water, and pat dry.

Add just enough oil to a large, preferably nonstick skillet to barely cover the bottom of the pan, and heat over medium heat. Add the garlic cloves and red pepper flakes, and cook, stirring about 1 minute to flavor the oil. Remove and discard the garlic. Increase the heat, add the zucchini to the skillet, and cook, turning once, until golden brown on each side. Work in batches so that the zucchini is in one layer in the skillet, adding more oil if necessary with each batch. The oil should be hot enough to brown the zucchini after 2 minutes or so, but not smoking, so watch the heat and adjust accordingly.

Transfer the cooked zucchini to a shallow dish, sprinkle with the mint and red wine vinegar, and season to taste with more salt. Serve immediately, or keep covered at room temperature for up to 6 hours.

YIELD: **4 TO 6** SERVINGS

- 4 to 6 medium-size zucchini, cut lengthwise into $1/4$-inch (6 mm) thick slices
- 2 tablespoons (36 g) kosher salt
- Olive oil
- 3 cloves garlic
- $1/2$ teaspoon red pepper flakes, or to taste
- $1/4$ cup (24 g) thinly sliced fresh mint leaves
- Red wine vinegar, to taste

Escabeche or *alla scapece* is a way of cooking meat, seafood, or vegetables by marinating after, rather than before, cooking and serving at room temperature. It's a technique likely Persian in origin that travelled to Europe with the Moors.

❧ Southern Minestrone ❧

Italian minestrone is a classic, comforting soup ideal for cool nights in late summer or fall. This Southern take includes lima beans and collard greens instead of the classic white beans and kale. Zucchini are a traditional addition, and give the soup a creamy texture.

After soaking the beans overnight in lightly salted water, rinse, drain, and set aside.

Bring the 10 cups (2.4 L) of water to a boil, reduce to a gentle simmer, cover, and set aside.

Cook the pasta separately in boiling salted water, and remove from heat about 2 minutes before the pasta would be fully cooked. Drain and set aside.

Purée the bacon and garlic together in a food processor (or finely mince). Heat the oil in a large, heavy stockpot over medium heat. Add the puréed bacon and garlic and cook, stirring frequently, 2 minutes. Add the onion and cook

2 more minutes. Add the tomato paste and cook 1 to 2 minutes, or until lightly browned. Add the potato, red pepper flakes, bay leaves, and thyme, and cook, stirring frequently, 2 to 4 minutes.

Add the carrot, celery, simmering 10 cups (2.4 L) water, and lima beans, and bring to a boil. Reduce to a simmer and cook, uncovered, about 30 minutes, or until the beans are halfway cooked. Add the collard greens and zucchini, and cook about 20 minutes, or until the vegetables are all very tender. Remove the bay leaves. Stir in the pasta just before serving. Season to taste with salt and pepper. Serve with Parmesan cheese, if desired.

YIELD: 6 TO 8 SERVINGS

1 cup (178 g) dried lima beans, soaked overnight in lightly salted water

10 cups (2.4 L) water, plus more for cooking the pasta

1/4 pound (115 g) ditalini pasta

4 slices thick-cut bacon, roughly chopped

3 cloves garlic

2 tablespoons (28 ml) olive oil

1 yellow onion, diced

2 tablespoons (32 g) tomato paste

1 large russet potato, peeled and diced

1/2 teaspoon red pepper flakes

2 bay leaves

1 tablespoon (2.4 g) fresh thyme leaves

1 medium-size carrot, diced

1 rib celery, diced

4 medium-size collard green leaves, stemmed and cut into 1-inch (2.5 cm) squares

2 medium-size zucchini, chopped

Salt and pepper

Optional garnish:

Parmesan cheese

Minestrone is a traditional but varied Italian soup made with beans, broth, pasta, and seasonal vegetables such as zucchini, potatoes, tomatoes, kale, and cabbage. It likely originated as a catchall dish made with whatever leftovers were on hand.

❧ Squash Tempura with Soy Dipping Sauce ❧

Zucchini is especially good fried, as frying locks in its moisture and gives it a creamy texture. Here, zucchini are fried tempura-style and served with a traditional dipping sauce.

To make the dashi: Place the kombu and water in a large stockpot, and bring to a simmer over medium-high heat. Just before the water boils, discard the kombu. Add the bonito flakes, bring back to a boil, and turn off the heat. Allow the flakes to settle to the bottom of the pan, then strain the broth with a fine-mesh strainer.

To make the dipping sauce: Mix together three-quarters of the dashi, mirin, and soy sauce in a saucepan, and bring to a simmer. Cover and set aside.

To make the tempura: Cut off and discard the ends of the squash, and slice crosswise into 2- to 3-inch (5 to 7.5 cm) sections. Cut each section in half lengthwise, in half lengthwise again, and then those in half lengthwise again. Transfer the squash to a colander, and generously season with the salt. (This is more salt than you would normally use, but some of the salt will penetrate, and some will be rinsed off.) Toss to coat with the salt, set aside for 20 to 30 minutes, then rinse well, and dry thoroughly with a kitchen towel.

When ready to fry, fill a large, heavy saucepan or skillet no more than halfway up the sides with oil, to a depth of at least 1 inch (2.5 cm). Heat the oil to 350°F (180°C). A little batter dripped into the oil should bubble at the surface.

Make the batter in two batches as you fry the zucchini to ensure it's as light as possible. For one batch of batter, lightly beat one egg in a shallow bowl, stir in 1 cup (235 ml) of the ice water, and add 1 cup (110 g) of the flour. Stir until the batter just comes together. There should be lumps in the batter; otherwise it will be tough. Repeat when ready to make the second batch.

Place the squash, 2 cups (220 g) of the flour for coating, and the batter in shallow bowls. Dip the zucchini into the flour, shake off the excess, then dip it into the batter, letting the loose batter drain away, then transfer it to the hot oil. Fry the squash in batches, without overcrowding the pan. Fry each batch, stirring gently once or twice with a slotted spoon, for 4 to 6 minutes, or until light golden and cooked through in the center.

Transfer the squash to a wire rack to drain, and sprinkle lightly with salt. Serve immediately alongside the dipping sauce, or if need be, keep the cooked squash warm in the oven on low heat.

YIELD: **4** TO **6** SERVINGS

For the dashi:

1 piece kombu (dried seaweed)

6 cups (1.4 L) water

2 cups (190 g) bonito flakes

For the dipping sauce:

¾ cup (175 ml) dashi or water

½ cup (120 ml) mirin

½ cup (120 ml) light soy sauce

For the tempura:

8 to 10 zucchini or straight-neck yellow squash, 4- to 6-inches (10 to 15 cm) long each

2 to 4 teaspoons (12 to 24 g) kosher salt

Canola oil, for frying

2 egg yolks, divided

2 cups (475 ml) ice water, divided

4 cups (440 g) sifted all-purpose flour, divided

❦ Summer Squash and Herb Gratin ❧

As far as gratins go, this one is pretty light, inspired by the summer bounty of Provence. Fresh Mediterranean herbs, butter, a smattering of bread crumbs, and Parmesan add lots of flavor, but those accents are simple enough that the fresh flavors of the squash come through.

Cut the squash into ¼-inch (6 mm) thick rounds, then cut the rounds in half. Place the squash in a colander and generously season with the 2 to 4 (12 to 24 g) teaspoons kosher salt to draw the excess moisture away from the squash. (This is more salt than you would normally season them with for eating. Some of the salt will penetrate, but some will be rinsed off.) Let sit 20 minutes, rinse with cold water, then thoroughly dry with a kitchen towel.

Preheat the oven to 400°F (200°C, or gas mark 6).

Heat 2 tablespoons (28 g) of the butter in medium-size skillet over medium heat. When the butter melts, swirl the pan for 2 to 4 minutes, or until the butter is lightly browned. Add the bread crumbs and cook, stirring constantly, 2 to 4 minutes, or until the bread crumbs are browned. Transfer to a bowl, and stir in ¼ cup (25 g) of the Parmesan.

Heat the olive oil and remaining 2 tablespoons (28 g) butter in a large ovenproof skillet over medium-high heat. Add the squash and garlic and cook, stirring often, 6 to 8 minutes, or until the squash is tender and brown in spots. Remove the pan from the heat, and stir in the remaining 1 cup (100 g) of Parmesan, the red pepper flakes, marjoram, rosemary, and parsley, and season to taste with black pepper.

Transfer the squash to a shallow gratin dish, top with the Parmesan and bread crumb mixture, and bake 20 to 30 minutes, or until hot and bubbly.

YIELD: **4** TO **6** SERVINGS

- 3 pounds (1.4 g) zucchini, yellow squash, or a combination
- 2 to 4 teaspoons (12 to 24 g) kosher salt, plus more to taste
- 4 tablespoons (55 g) unsalted butter, divided
- ½ cup (60 g) panko bread crumbs
- 1¼ (125 g) cup freshly grated Parmesan, divided
- 2 tablespoons (28 ml) olive oil
- 4 cloves garlic, sliced
- 1 teaspoon (1.2 g) red pepper flakes
- 2 teaspoons (1.2 g) minced fresh marjoram
- 1 teaspoon (0.7 g) minced fresh rosemary
- 2 teaspoons (2.6 g) minced fresh parsley
- Freshly ground black pepper

A gratin is a dish of French origin usually consisting of vegetables but sometimes meat or seafood, layered in a shallow dish, and topped with a combination of bread crumbs and various cheeses, and baked or broiled to make the topping crisp.

❧ Baby Squash and Blossoms with Goat Cheese and Basil ❧

This dish is best with zucchini that are no more than 2-inches (5 cm) long. Any longer and they won't be cooked by the time the goat cheese is hot and bubbly. If the squash you have are bigger, use only the blossoms and save the zucchini for another dish. Any baby summer squash will work here.

14 to 16 baby zucchini or other summer squash with blossoms attached (about 1 pound, or 455 g)

12 ounces (340 g) fresh goat cheese, chilled

10 to 12 fresh basil leaves, very thinly sliced

$\frac{1}{2}$ teaspoon Maldon or other coarse salt, plus more to taste

Olive oil

Preheat the oven to 400°F (200°C, or gas mark 6).

Trim the tough stem end off the squash, and discard it. Leaving the blossom end of the squash intact, slice the squash almost in half lengthwise, and then slice each half almost in half again lengthwise so that the blossoms are attached to a kind of "butterflied" squash split into four attached lengths. Carefully open up the blossoms by slicing them open along one side.

Place the goat cheese, basil, and salt in a bowl, and stir to combine. Using a small spoon, place 1 tablespoon (9 g) or so of the goat cheese into the bottom of each blossom. Wrap the blossom around the cheese, enclosing to secure the cheese within the blossom.

Arrange the squash and stuffed blossoms on a large sheet pan lined with a silicone baking mat or parchment paper. Drizzle evenly with olive oil, getting some of the oil in between the sliced zucchini. Season the squash lightly with salt. Bake 8 to 12 minutes, or until the cheese is hot but not melting away. Transfer the zucchini to a platter immediately, and serve.

YIELD: **4** TO **6** SERVINGS

∂ **Bowtie Pasta with Guanciale, Yellow Squash, and Pinto Beans** ℰ

The combination of pork, squash, and beans is one of my favorites, especially in comforting dishes such as pastas. Pinto beans and yellow squash instead of the more classic Italian zucchini and white beans lend Southern flavor to this dish. If you don't have guanciale (cured pork jowl), you can substitute bacon or pancetta.

⅓ pound (150 g) bowtie pasta

2 tablespoons (28 ml) olive oil

3 ounces (85 g) guanciale, diced

1 medium-size shallot, diced

½ teaspoon red pepper flakes

3 medium-size yellow squash (about 1½ pounds, or 680 g), sliced

1 medium-size tomato, chopped, or 1 cup (250 g) tomato purée

1½ cups (257 g) cooked pinto beans, or 1 can (15 ounces, or 425 g), rinsed and drained

3 tablespoons (12 g) chopped fresh parsley

½ cup (100 g) Parmesan

Cook the pasta according to the package directions in generously salted boiling water. Reserve 1 cup (235 ml) of the pasta cooking water.

Meanwhile, heat the olive oil and guanciale in a large skillet over medium-high heat. When the oil is hot, add the shallot and pepper flakes. Cook, stirring often, 2 to 4 minutes, or until the guanciale starts to brown.

Add the squash and cook, stirring often, 4 to 6 minutes, or until the squash begins to turn tender. Add the tomato, pinto beans, and ½ cup (120 ml) of the pasta cooking water. Simmer, stirring once or twice, until the tomato breaks down and the squash is tender, adding a little more of the pasta water if necessary. There should be 1 to 2 tablespoons (15 to 28 ml) of liquid in the bottom of the pan just before adding the pasta; to adjust, add more pasta cooking water if there's not enough, or increase the heat if there's too much.

Drain the pasta and add it to the sauce. Cook 1 to 2 minutes, stirring until the pasta is coated with the thickened sauce and vegetables. Turn off the heat, stir in the parsley and Parmesan, and serve.

YIELD: **4** TO **6** SERVINGS

❧ Chicken, Squash, Corn, and Poblano Tacos ❧

Cumin, coriander, and fennel seed give these simple tacos great flavor. Use ground spices if that's all you have, but toasting whole spices in a dry skillet about 5 minutes until fragrant, then grinding them in a dedicated spice grinder or mortar and pestle (or even by putting them in a resealable plastic bag and crushing with the bottom of a skillet) makes for much better flavor.

Season the chicken generously on both sides with salt, and then lightly sprinkle with cayenne pepper. Place the chicken in a medium-size saucepan, and add the butter and just enough water to cover. Cover, and cook the chicken at a bare simmer, about 20 to 30 minutes, or until cooked through (an instant-read thermometer inserted in the thickest part should read 150°F, or 65°C). Turn off the heat and set the saucepan aside to keep the chicken warm.

Heat the canola oil in a large skillet over medium heat. Add the onion, poblanos, cumin, coriander, fennel, and ½ teaspoon salt (less if you're using chicken stock), and cook, stirring frequently, 3 to 5 minutes. Add the garlic and cook 30 seconds. Add the tomato purée, water or chicken stock, and squash, and cook, stirring occasionally, 8 to 10 minutes, or until the squash are almost tender. Add more water or chicken stock during cooking as necessary. There should be enough liquid to make for a stew consistency. Season to taste with salt.

Transfer the chicken to a cutting board and shred with two forks. Add the shredded chicken and the corn to the zucchini mixture, stir to combine, and simmer just to warm through. Stir in the cilantro and crema, and season to taste with salt and cayenne pepper.

Serve with the cheese, lime wedges, and tortillas.

YIELD: **4** SERVINGS OF **4** TACOS EACH

1 boneless, skinless chicken breast half

Kosher salt

Cayenne pepper

2 tablespoons (28 g) unsalted butter

1½ tablespoons (25 ml) canola oil

1 medium-size yellow onion, diced

2 medium-size poblano chiles, diced

2 teaspoons ground cumin

1 teaspoon (2 g) ground coriander

½ teaspoon ground fennel seed

½ teaspoon kosher salt

1 clove garlic, minced

1 cup (250 g) tomato purée, or 1 can (15 ounces, or 430 g) whole, peeled tomatoes, puréed

1 cup (235 ml) water or chicken stock, plus more as needed

4 medium-size (zucchini or yellow) squash, cut into ½-inch (13 mm) cubes

1 cup (136 g) fresh sweet corn

2 to 4 tablespoons (2 to 4 g) chopped fresh cilantro

½ cup (115 g) Mexican crema, crème fraîche, or sour cream

2 to 3 cups (150 to 225 g) queso fresco or feta cheese

Lime wedges

16 corn tortillas, warmed

❧ Stir-Fried Beef, Zucchini, and Sweet Onions ❧

This is a simple, Chinese-inspired stir-fry with a sauce that works well with a number of ingredient combinations. Here, beef, zucchini, and onions are particularly good together, with the high heat sealing in the zucchini's moisture, and the beef and onions lending hearty, grounding flavor. Sesame seeds are traditional to both Southern and Asian cuisines, and basil adds an aromatic top note of flavor at the end of cooking.

Season the sliced beef all over with salt and pepper, and set aside, for at least 30 minutes and up to 1 hour. In a small bowl, whisk together the bean sauce, soy sauce, chili sauce, wine or sherry, water, ginger, garlic, and cornstarch, and set aside.

Heat half the oil in a large, heavy, nonstick skillet over high heat. Pat the beef dry with a paper towel. When the oil is hot, add the beef to the pan and cook, stirring occasionally, 1 to 2 minutes, or until browned. Transfer the beef to a bowl.

Add the remaining oil to the skillet, along with the onion and zucchini. Cook, stirring occasionally, 2 to 4 minutes, or until the zucchini is browned. Add a splash of water to the pan, stir, and cook another 2 to 4 minutes, or until the zucchini is tender.

Add the beef and any accumulated juices to the pan, and toss to combine. Cook 1 to 2 minutes, or until the beef is just cooked through. Add the sauce and cook, stirring frequently, 1 to 2 minutes, or until the sauce thickens. Stir in the basil and the sesame seeds, if desired. Season to taste with salt and pepper.

YIELD: 2 SERVINGS

½ pound (225 g) beef filet, strip, or other tender cut, thinly sliced

Kosher salt

Freshly ground black pepper

1 tablespoon (15 ml) Chinese ground bean sauce or black bean sauce

2 teaspoons (10 ml) soy sauce

1 teaspoon (5 g) sambal oelek chili sauce or hot sauce

1 tablespoon (15 ml) Shaoxing wine or dry sherry

3 tablespoons (45 ml) water

1 teaspoon (2 g) minced ginger

1 clove garlic, minced

1 teaspoon (3 g) cornstarch

1 tablespoon (15 ml) canola oil, divided

1 sweet onion, sliced

3 medium-size zucchini, thinly sliced

3 to 5 basil leaves, torn into pieces

1 tablespoon (8 g) black sesame seeds (optional)

COLLARD GREENS

As a child, I mostly knew collards as that wet mess of overcooked greens in a small bowl alongside chicken or pork chops in a country-style meat-and-three (a casual, country-style restaurant common in the South, usually serving a choice of one meat dish and a choice of three vegetable dishes). At home, we always seemed to prefer spinach and cabbage. Traveling in France, Italy, and the Middle East years later and seeing how folks cooked with chard and kale, I realized collards could be incorporated into all kinds of dishes in the same quick-cook way as those greens.

Since moving to the Lowcountry, where collards grow year-round in the moderate climate and sandy soils of the sea islands (including in my garden on Sullivan's Island), I've made collards one of my staple greens. They do well in both the heat and the cold, unlike other greens with more delicate leaves. They tend to be sweeter in the colder months after they've gone through a frost, and they are usually less bitter than mustard greens, turnip greens, and broccoli rabe, though more so than chard and kale. They usually take a little longer to cook than those greens because their leaves are sturdier, and younger collards with smaller leaves cook pretty quickly.

Like most greens, collards are a natural match with beans, legumes, and pork. Collards have an assertive flavor and texture, so they benefit from strongly flavored ingredients that can stand up to that boldness: spices, fresh herbs, mushrooms, tomatoes, and aged cheeses such as Parmesan. For that reason, collards have been incorporated into cooking in tropical and Mediterranean climates—Brazil, Kenya, Portugal, Kashmir—that favor assertive flavors.

The classic Southern way to cook collards is to boil them for a long time in water with one of the less sought-after cuts of smoked pork such as neck or fatback. When done right—it's a classic for a reason—the resulting "pot likker" is as esteemed as the greens themselves. But more often than not, I try to retain the collards' color, texture, and nutrients by cooking them more quickly with less liquid. I love them quickly sautéed with a sweeter green such as chard or, as a snack, just tossed with a little olive oil and roasted until crispy.

At the market, choose the smallest collard greens you can find. Store them unwashed, wrapped in damp paper towels in a perforated paper or plastic bag, and they'll keep up to a week. Since they tend to grow in sandy soils and can become gritty, clean collards well by swishing them around in a sink full of water then lifting them out to drain. I almost always cut out and discard the leaves' central stem, either with two quick slices along both sides of the stem or by folding the leaves in half and tearing or slicing the stem right off.

❧ Crispy Roasted Collards ❧

Since collards are a sturdy green, they're a good candidate for roasting. The high heat of the oven zaps their moisture and concentrates their flavor. Keep an eye on them as they cook since they can burn quickly in the high heat.

1½ pounds (683 g) collard greens, stems removed

¼ teaspoon kosher salt

2 teaspoons (10 ml) olive oil

Preheat the oven to 425°F (220°C, or gas mark 7).

Cut the leaves in half lengthwise then cut each half into 2- to 3-inch (5 to 7.5 cm) pieces. Combine all ingredients in a large bowl, and toss to coat the collards. Spread the collards out on a large sheet pan, and roast for 5 to 10 minutes, or until pieces are crisp and brown in spots.

YIELD: **4** TO **6** SERVINGS

❧ Collards with Garlic and Mustard Seeds ❧

The thinly sliced collards in this simple sauté are inspired by a traditional Brazilian preparation, but the flavors are inspired by both India and the Deep South. Since the greens are so thin, they don't need to cook the typical Southern hour or two, which means they hold on to their nutrients, too.

3 tablespoons (45 ml) vegetable oil

1 tablespoon (11 g) mustard seeds

1 small shallot, thinly sliced

1 teaspoon (1.2 g) red pepper flakes

6 cloves garlic, thinly sliced

1 ½ pounds (683 g) collard greens, stems cut away and discarded, leaves cut into thin strips

Salt and freshly ground black pepper

Heat the oil in a large skillet over medium-high heat. Add the mustard seeds, and cover the skillet since the mustard seeds will pop. When the mustard seeds are done popping, after 1 or 2 minutes, reduce the heat to medium. Add the shallot and red pepper flakes and cook, stirring frequently, 2 to 4 minutes, or until the shallots are light brown. Add the garlic and stir 1 to 2 minutes, or until light brown. Stir in the collard greens and cook, stirring frequently, 6 to 8 minutes, or until the collards are bright green and wilted. Add a splash of water if necessary to help the collards cook and to keep the garlic from getting too brown. Season to taste with salt and pepper.

YEILD: 4 TO 6 SERVINGS

❧ Quick-Cooked Collards, Chard, and Escarole ❧

In this mix of greens, collards are on the earthy side, chard is a little sweeter, and escarole has a pleasing bitterness. When cooked together, each of these flavor notes joins the others to make a harmonious chord. Soy sauce and rice vinegar are the bottom and top notes.

Heat the olive oil in a large skillet over medium-high heat. Add the garlic and ginger, and stir about 30 seconds, until fragrant. Add the collard greens and cook, stirring frequently, 2 to 4 minutes. Add the chard and escarole, and stir another 2 to 4 minutes, or until the greens are tender. Stir in the red pepper flakes, soy sauce, and rice vinegar, and season to taste with salt and pepper.

YIELD: **4** TO **6** SERVINGS

4 teaspoons (20 ml) olive oil

2 cloves garlic, thinly sliced

4 teaspoons (8 g) minced fresh ginger

8 ounces (227 g) each collard greens, Swiss chard, and escarole, stems cut away and discarded, leaves cut into pieces

½ teaspoons red pepper flakes

4 teaspoons (20 ml) soy sauce

4 teaspoons (20 ml) rice wine vinegar

Salt and freshly ground black pepper

❧ Collards with Peppers, Currants, and Pine Nuts ❧

From Rome southward, Italian cooks like to experiment with the combination of sweet, sour, and bitter. This trio of greens, raisins or currants, and nuts is a typical combination in Sicily, and works well with the slightly bitter collards.

Toast the pine nuts in a dry skillet over medium heat, stirring often, 2 to 4 minutes, or until lightly toasted. Place the currants in a bowl, cover with boiling water, and let steep 5 minutes. Drain.

Heat 1 tablespoon (15 ml) of the olive oil in a large skillet over medium-high heat. When hot, add the onion, bell peppers, red pepper flakes, and a pinch of salt, and cook, stirring often, 2 to 4 minutes, or until the vegetables are softened. Transfer to a plate.

Add the remaining 1 tablespoon (15 ml) olive oil to the same skillet over medium-high heat. Add the collard greens and another pinch of salt, and cook, stirring frequently, 4 to 6 minutes, or until the greens are wilted.

Return the onions, bell peppers, pine nuts, and currants to the skillet. Cook 6 to 8 minutes, or until the collard greens are tender. Season to taste with salt and pepper.

YIELD: **4** TO **6** SERVINGS

1/4 cup (35 g) pine nuts

1/4 cups (38 g) dried currants

2 tablespoons (30 ml) olive oil, divided

1/2 yellow onion, thinly sliced

2 red bell peppers, thinly sliced

1/4 teaspoon red pepper flakes

Salt

1 1/2 pounds (683 g) collard greens, stems removed and discarded, leaves cut into 1/2-inch (13 mm) squares

Freshly ground black pepper

❧ Lamb-Stuffed Collards ❧

In this dish, collard greens are stuffed in the Mediterranean style. The lamb and bulgur combination is a nice match with the greens, and the tomato sauce lends contrasting brightness.

To make the stuffed collards: Bring the 4 cups of water to a boil, stir in the salt and bulgur, and then lower the heat to simmer gently 10 to 15 minutes, or until the bulgur is tender. Drain, rinse the bulgur with cold water, and set aside until completely drained, stirring occasionally to help this process along.

While the bulgur is cooking, prepare the collard leaves by peeling the central stems with a vegetable peeler so that they're flush with the leaves. Cut off the stem ends below the leaves and discard.

Bring a large stockpot of generously salted water to a boil. Working in two batches, add the collard green leaves, and blanch about 2 minutes, or until bright green but still firm. Transfer the leaves to a kitchen towel to drain.

Heat the olive oil in large skillet over medium-high heat. Add the onion, season lightly with salt, and cook, stirring often, 3 to 5 minutes, or until translucent. Add the garlic and cook about 30 seconds until fragrant.

Add the ground lamb and oregano, season with salt and pepper, and add the red pepper flakes. Cook, stirring often and breaking the lamb up, 10 to 15 minutes, or until meat is cooked through. Stir in the mint and lemon zest.

Transfer the lamb mixture to a large bowl, leaving about 1 tablespoon (15 ml) of fat in the skillet. Add the bulgur to the bowl with the lamb, stir to combine, and season to taste with salt and pepper.

To make the sauce: Return the skillet to medium-high heat, and add the onion. Cook for 3 to 5 minutes, or until translucent. Add the garlic, and cook about 30 seconds until fragrant. Add the tomatoes and cook, stirring and breaking them up, about 10 minutes, or until it thickens to a sauce. Season to taste with salt, black pepper, and red pepper flakes. Stir one-fourth of this tomato sauce into the lamb and bulgur mixture.

To assemble: Preheat the oven to 375°F (190°C, or gas mark 5).

Spread out the collard leaves on a work surface. Divide the lamb and bulgur mixture among the collard leaves, mounding it in the center. Roll each collard leaf over the lamb mixture, folding the sides inward.

Cover the bottom of a large casserole dish with half of the remaining tomato sauce, top with the stuffed collards, and spread the remaining tomato sauce over the collards. Pour the wine into the bottom of the casserole dish, cover with foil, and bake about 30 minutes.

YIELD: **4** TO **6** SERVINGS

For the stuffed collards:

4 cups (945 ml) water, plus more for blanching the collards

½ teaspoon kosher salt, plus more to taste

¾ cup (105 g) bulgur

12 ounces (340 g) collard green leaves (about 8 to 10 medium-size leaves)

1 tablespoon (15 ml) olive oil

½ medium yellow onion, diced

1 cloves garlic, minced

2 pounds (905 g) ground lamb

2 teaspoons (2 g) dried oregano

Freshly ground black pepper

½ teaspoon red pepper flakes

4 to 6 fresh mint leaves, thinly sliced

1 teaspoon (2 g) freshly grated lemon zest

For the sauce:

½ medium-size yellow onion, diced

1 cloves garlic, minced

1 can (28 ounces, or 795 g) whole peeled tomatoes

Kosher salt

Freshly ground black pepper

Red pepper flakes

1 cup (235 ml) dry white wine

ℑ Chicken, Collard, and Country Ham Saltimbocca ℰ

In Italy, you'll see classic saltimbocca elevated with chopped spinach, but collards, where they are plentiful and seasonal, work well too. Rather than prosciutto, country ham substitutes and gives this saltimbocca a southern hominess.

Cook the collard leaves in generously salted boiling water 2 to 4 minutes, or until leaves are bright green. Drain, squeeze out any excess liquid from the leaves, and finely chop them.

Preheat the oven to 350°F (180°C, or gas mark 4). Place a shallow 11 x 7 x 2-inch (28 x 18 x 5 cm) baking dish on the middle rack of the oven to preheat.

Cut the chicken breast halves in half crosswise to make roughly triangular portions. Cover with plastic wrap and pound to an even thickness (about ⅛ inch, or 3 mm). Season the chicken on both sides with salt and pepper. Divide the chopped collards equally among the chicken, spreading evenly over each piece. Spoon the Parmesan cheese over the collards, and top the cheese with a piece of country ham. Roll each portion up tightly, top each with a sage leaf, and secure with a toothpick.

Heat the olive oil in a large skillet over medium-high heat. Add the chicken to the skillet and cook, turning with tongs to brown, about 6 to 8 minutes total. Transfer the chicken to the preheated casserole dish. Set aside the skillet, reserving the chicken juices. Add enough white wine to the casserole dish to cover the bottom. Place the dish in the oven, and cook 8 to 10 minutes, or until the chicken is just cooked through.

Return the skillet to medium-high heat. Add the ¾ cup (175 ml) of stock and the lemon juice to the skillet and cook, scraping the bottom of the pan, until liquid is reduced by one quarter. Meanwhile, make a slurry by whisking together the remaining 2 tablespoons (30 ml) of the stock and the cornstarch.

Add the butter and stir to incorporate it into the sauce, then stir in the cornstarch slurry. Cook about 30 seconds, or until the sauce boils and thickens. Spoon the sauce over the chicken. Serve with the lemon wedges, if desired

YIELD: **4 SERVINGS**

4 ounces (115 g) collard greens, stems removed and discarded

2 boneless, skinless chicken breast halves

Salt and freshly ground black pepper

¼ cup (20 g) freshly grated Parmesan cheese, or to taste

4 thin slices sugar-cured country ham

4 fresh sage leaves

1 tablespoon (15 ml) olive oil

1 cup (235 ml) dry white wine

¾ cup plus 2 tablespoons (205 ml) chicken stock, divided

2 tablespoons (30 ml) fresh lemon juice

1 teaspoon (3 g) cornstarch

2 tablespoons (28 g) unsalted butter

Optional garnish:

Lemon wedges

Saltimbocca means "jumps in the mouth" in Italian and is popular in Rome. It's made with veal or chicken topped with ham or prosciutto and sage, panfried, and topped with a pan sauce made with lemon or wine and often capers.

❧ Collard, Corn, Black Bean, and Mushroom Quesadillas ❧

I'd put just about anything in between a folded tortilla and top it with cheese, but this is an especially good combination. The slightly chewy texture of the collards with melted jack cheese, mushrooms, and black beans match with the collards' earthiness, and corn lends a nice textural pop and sweetness.

Cook the collard leaves in a large stockpot of generously salted boiling water for 2 to 4 minutes, or until the leaves are bright green. Drain, squeeze out any excess liquid from the leaves, and finely chop them.

Heat 1 tablespoon (15 ml) of the olive oil in a large nonstick skillet over medium-high heat. Add the paprika, cumin, and coriander, and cook, stirring constantly, 1 minute. Add the mushrooms and cook, stirring often, 2 to 4 minutes, or until tender. Add the collard greens and black beans, and cook 2 to 4 minutes, or until mixture is hot. Transfer this mixture to a bowl, and wipe the skillet out with a paper towel.

Divide the collard mixture among the tortillas. Top with the cheese, and fold the quesadillas in half, pressing to enclose the filling.

Heat half the remaining 1 tablespoon (15 ml) of olive oil in the same skillet over medium heat. When hot, add the quesadillas in batches, two at a time if there is room, and cook, turning once, 3 to 4 minutes on each side, or until brown on the outside and hot on the inside. Serve with hot sauce, avocado, and sour cream, if desired.

YIELD: **4** SERVINGS

1 pound (455 g) collard greens, stems removed and discarded, leaves cut into 1/2-inch squares

Kosher salt

2 tablespoons (28 ml) olive oil, divided

1 teaspoon (2.5 g) smoked paprika

2 teaspoons (2.5 g) ground cumin

2 teaspoons (2 g) ground coriander

6 ounces (170 g) shiitake mushrooms, stems removed and discarded, thinly sliced

2 cups (344 g) cooked black beans

4 flour tortillas, 8 to 10 inches (20 to 25 cm) each

2 cups (240 g) grated Monterey Jack or queso Oaxaca

Optional garnishes:

Hot sauce

Sliced avocado

Sour cream

❦ Collard and Feta Pie ❧

This is a Southern take on spanakopita, a Greek spinach and feta pie that I associate with Christmas day at my grandparents' house. Birmingham has a vibrant Greek community, and many of the city's Greek families started catering companies and would help us with get-togethers during the holidays, serving Southern-inspired Greek food. The collards are a natural substitute for spinach in this dish, their hearty texture standing up to the rich buttery flavor and crispy texture of the pie.

4 pounds (1.8 kg) collard greens, stems removed, leaves cut into 1/2-inch squares

9 tablespoons (126 g) unsalted butter, divided

1 tablespoon (15 ml) olive oil

1 large yellow onion, diced

4 scallions, thinly sliced, white and green parts separated

1/2 teaspoon kosher salt

1 cup (60 g) loosely packed fresh parsley leaves, chopped

1 cup (9 g) fresh dill, chopped

1/8 teaspoon freshly grated nutmeg

1 pound (455 g) feta cheese, crumbled

1/2 cup (50 g) grated Parmesan

1/2 cup (125 g) ricotta cheese

2 eggs, lightly beaten

4 ounces (120 ml) olive oil

20 frozen phyllo sheets, thawed in the refrigerator

Cook the collard leaves in generously salted boiling water for 2 to 4 minutes, or until leaves are bright green. Drain, squeeze out any excess liquid from the leaves, and finely chop them.

Melt 1 tablespoon (14 g) of the butter and the olive oil in a large skillet over medium heat. When the butter's foam subsides, add the onion, the white parts of the scallions, and the salt, and cook for 5 minutes without browning. Add the chopped collards, the green parts of the scallions, and the parsley, dill, and nutmeg. Stir to combine and cook for 5 more minutes.

In a large bowl, combine the feta, Parmesan, ricotta, and eggs. Stir well, mashing any big chunks of feta with the back of a fork.

Preheat the oven to 375°F (190°C, or gas mark 5).

Add the collard mixture to the cheese mixture, stir to combine, and set aside.

To assemble the pie, melt the remaining 8 tablespoons (112 g) of butter and mix together with the olive oil. Lightly grease a 13 x 9 x 2-inch (33 x 23 x 5 cm) baking dish with some of the butter and oil mixture. For the bottom layer of the pie, place ten phyllo sheets into the dish, brushing the top of each phyllo sheet with the butter and oil mixture as you go, and allowing the overhanging edges to come up the sides of the dish.

Evenly spread the collard-cheese mixture on top of the phyllo sheets. Layer the remaining ten phyllo sheets on top of the spinach-cheese mixture, brushing the top of each sheet with the butter-oil mixture. Tuck the edges of the phyllo in around the sides of the dish and lightly score the top layer into 3-inch (7.5 cm) squares. Bake about 45 minutes, or until the top layer is golden brown and flaky. Cool before cutting.

YIELD: **6 TO 8 SERVINGS**

ẾP THÁI

0000

NẾP BẮC
2 8000

NẾP NGỒ
2200

THÁI LÀI DẺO
16000

Đ

M

THƠM THÁI MỀ
15000

ÊN CHỢ ĐÀO
000

RICE

When we were growing up, I remember my dad at the dinner table, waxing eloquent on the minimal beauty of a simple pile of white rice with nothing on it but a pat of butter and lots of freshly ground black pepper. It's a simple way of serving rice tailored to the sweetness of varieties such as California Gold and might be the closest thing there is to an honest taste of the South.

Since rice supplies nutrition for a big portion of the world's population, calling it quintessentially Southern is a stretch. Even so, rice's popularity now and for the ages is precisely why it has had such a lasting impact on the South, probably more so than any other crop. In the eighteenth century, the Lowcountry between Savannah, Georgia, and Georgetown, South Carolina, with Charleston at its heart, supplied a large percentage of the world's rice.

Charleston's most beautiful buildings were built on the profits from rice and on the backs of slaves from Africa and the Caribbean, who brought with them culinary traditions that fused with those of the French Huguenots, who carried across the Atlantic the rice pilafs and other dishes that were French in origin but had deeper roots in the Middle East and Persia. No other crop has had such a pivotal role in influencing, and even creating, the South.

Of course, rice is pivotal to cuisines around the globe—to the paellas of Spain; the risottos, *arrancini*, and *suppli* of Italy; to the seemingly endless variations of chicken and rice dishes found the world over, from the Caribbean and Mexico to the Middle East to Singapore. I've swooned over rice noodle soups and spring rolls in Vietnam; sweet rice desserts in Thailand; and Cajun and Creole rice dishes of all kinds in New Orleans and the Florida Panhandle. And in Egypt, I was nursed back to health by a dish called *kushari*, which consisted of tomato-infused rice, lentils, and fried onions, served in a Styrofoam cup.

While white rice, which has had the chaff and germ removed for easier shipping and storage, is the most widely available rice variety, I also like to seek out interesting whole grain types, such as Southeast Asian red rice, Chinese black forbidden rice, and Texan brown basmati. Short-grain Italian types, such as arborio and carnaroli, have exterior starches that lend creaminess to risottos. Fragrant Thai jasmine rice is an aromatic wonder alongside stir-fries, and stickier short-grain Japanese varieties are delicious with simple vegetable dishes, making them easy to eat with chopsticks.

❧ Carolina Gold Rice with Butter and Ground Black Pepper ❧

Carolina Gold is the variety of rice responsible for the Georgia and South Carolina Lowcountry's rise to prominence in the seventeenth century. Because of its creamy texture and indulgent flavor, this prized variety was known as Charleston Ice Cream. This method of cooking it is adapted from a recipe by Anson Mills, a grower and supplier of heirloom beans and grains.

6 cups (1.4 L) water

1 tablespoon (18 g) kosher salt

1 cup (185 g) Carolina Gold rice

3 tablespoons (42 g) unsalted butter

Black pepper

Preheat the oven to 350°F (180°C, or gas mark 4).

Bring water and the salt to a boil in a medium-size, heavy-bottom saucepan. Add the rice, stir, and bring to a boil again. Immediately reduce the heat and gently simmer, uncovered, stirring occasionally, about 15 minutes, or until the rice is barely tender.

Drain the rice in a colander, and rinse thoroughly with cold water. Allow any excess water to drain away. Evenly distribute the rice on a rimmed baking sheet. Bake, stirring with a spatula once or twice, 5 to 7 minutes, or until rice is almost dry. Transfer the rice to a serving dish, and dot with the butter. Season to taste with black pepper.

YIELD: 2 TO 4 SERVINGS

Red Beans and Rice with Pickled Pork

My friend Brad Norton grew up in Mississippi and has been cooking this family recipe since he can remember. Red beans are native to North America and were incorporated into the hodge-podge of Spanish, Southern, African, and Caribbean cooking that evolved in the Deep South and Florida, and have long been served over rice. The pickled pork addition in this version adds amazing depth of flavor.

To make the pickled pork: Combine all the ingredients except the pork itself, in a medium-size saucepan. Bring to a boil over high heat, then reduce the heat, and gently boil for 2 minutes. Remove the pan from the heat and let cool completely. Combine this pickling solution and the pork in a plastic or glass container and refrigerate, covered, for 72 hours. Drain, rinse, and chop the pork into ½-inch (13 mm) pieces.

To make the red beans: Combine the soaked beans and water in a stockpot and bring to a boil over high heat; reduce to a simmer, and cook, covered, 45 minutes.

Add the bell peppers, onions, scallions, garlic, andouille, celery, parsley, ketchup, tomatoes, allspice, Tabasco sauce, and the pickled pork. Cook, uncovered, stirring occasionally, 1½ hours, adding more water if necessary to keep all the ingredients submerged; skim off and discard any foam that rises to the surface.

Season the bean and pork mixture to taste with salt, and test the beans for doneness. If they're tender, use a wooden spoon to mash the beans, pork, and vegetables against the side of the pot to make a thickener, leaving about half the beans whole. For the right consistency, the red beans should be gravy-like. Before serving, stir in the white wine vinegar and season to taste with salt and pepper.

Cook the rice according to the package directions. Ladle the red beans over the rice, and serve with additional Tabasco sauce, if desired.

YIELD: 8 TO 10 SERVINGS

For the pickled pork:

6 cloves garlic, peeled and crushed

4 bay leaves

20 black peppercorns

3 tablespoons (22 g) mustard seeds

3 tablespoons (20 g) celery seeds

4 tablespoons (54 g) kosher salt

4 cups (945 ml) white vinegar

3 tablespoons (45 ml) Tabasco sauce

2 teaspoons (3.5 g) cayenne pepper

3 tablespoons (15 g) coriander seeds

1 pound (455 g) pork shoulder (Boston butt), cut into 2-inch (5 cm) pieces

For the red beans:

2 pounds (905 g) dried red kidney beans, soaked overnight in lightly salted water, drained and rinsed

3½ quarts (3.5 L) water

2 green bell peppers, chopped

2 yellow onions, chopped

2 bunches scallions, sliced

7 cloves garlic, minced

1 pound (455 g) smoked andouille links, cut into 1-inch (2.5 cm) cubes

1 cup (100 g) chopped celery

1 bunch parsley, chopped

1 cup (240 g) ketchup

3 fresh tomatoes, chopped

3 teaspoons (2 g) ground allspice

2 tablespoons (28 ml) Tabasco sauce

1 teaspoon (5 ml) white wine vinegar

Salt and ground black pepper

4 cups (740 g) long-grain white rice

Red beans and rice is a Louisiana Creole dish made with red beans stewed with the holy trinity of aromatics—onion, bell pepper, and garlic—plus cayenne pepper, thyme, bay leaf, and pork or chicken broth, and sometimes tasso ham and andouille sausage. Rice and bean dishes are common in the Caribbean and Central America. In northern India, rajma is a red beans and rice dish flavored with Indian spices.

❧ Red Rice, Chickpea, and Tomato Salad with Lemon, Cilantro, and Pecans ❧

I love trying the myriad varieties of rice available these days. This whole-grain red rice has amazing flavor, and it looks and tastes great in this simple summer salad. Like most grain-based salads, this one gets better after sitting for a while.

Toast the pecan pieces in a dry skillet over medium heat 2 to 4 minutes until fragrant, then coarsely chop.

Combine the rice, water, and 1 teaspoon (6 g) salt in a medium-size, heavy stockpot; bring to a boil, reduce to a simmer, cover, and cook until the rice is tender. Drain the rice in a colander, and rinse with cold water. Drain very well, stirring to help this process along.

In a large bowl, combine the rice with the tomatoes, chickpeas, lemon juice, olive oil, scallions, and cilantro. Season to taste with salt and pepper, and add more olive oil or lemon juice, if desired.

YIELD: **4** TO **6** SERVINGS

1 cup (100 g) pecans

2 cups (370 g) red rice

4 cups (945 ml) water

1 teaspoon (6 g) kosher salt, plus more to taste

2 cups (about 25) cherry tomatoes, halved

2 1/2 cups (480 g) cooked chickpeas, or 2 cans (15 ounces, or 430 g, each), rinsed and drained

4 tablespoons (60 ml) lemon juice

4 tablespoons (60 ml) olive oil

4 scallions, green parts only, thinly sliced (about 1/2 cup, or 35 g)

1 cup (16 g) loosely packed cilantro leaves, coarsely chopped

Salt and freshly ground black pepper

❧ Turkey, Brown Rice, and Feta-Stuffed Bell Peppers ❧

Vegetables stuffed with flavorful beef, pork, and lamb are common throughout the Mediterranean, from Spain to the Middle East. This version is made with ground turkey, but you can substitute ground beef or lamb if you like. The brown rice is an ideal canvas for the spices and cheese.

Preheat the oven to 400°F (200°C, or gas mark 6). Heat the olive oil in a large skillet over medium-high heat. When the oil is hot, add the onion, cumin, coriander, and salt. Cook 2 to 4 minutes, or until the onion softens. Stir in the garlic and paprika, and cook 1 minute. Add the ground turkey, stir and cook, breaking the turkey apart with a spoon, 10 to 15 minutes, or until the turkey is fully cooked.

Meanwhile place the bell peppers directly onto the oven rack. Bake them for 6 to 8 minutes, or until they start to turn soft, then transfer them to a cutting board to cool.

Stir the brown rice, crumbled halloumi, and parsley into the ground turkey mixture, and season to taste with salt and pepper.

Using a paring knife, carefully cut the top off of each of the peppers and pull or cut out the core. Spoon equal amounts of the turkey mixture into the peppers. Arrange the peppers in a deep casserole dish, standing upright. Pour the wine into the bottom of the casserole dish. Bake 45 to 60 minutes, or until the filling is hot and the peppers are soft and brown in spots.

YIELD: **6 TO 8** SERVINGS

- 6 tablespoons (90 ml) olive oil
- 1 yellow onion, diced
- 2 teaspoons (5 g) ground cumin
- 1 teaspoon (2 g) ground coriander
- 1 teaspoon (6 g) kosher salt, plus more to taste
- 2 cloves garlic, minced
- 1 tablespoon (7 g) smoked sweet paprika
- 1 pound (455 g) ground turkey
- 6 to 8 medium-size green bell peppers
- 1 1/2 cup (290 g) cooked and drained brown rice
- 1 cup (150 g) halloumi cheese, crumbled
- 1/2 cup (60 g) chopped fresh parsley
- Freshly ground black pepper
- 1 cup (235 ml) white wine

❧ Chard, Walnut, and Gorgonzola Risotto ❧

This is a northern Italian take on risotto, one that might be served as a *primi* ("first course") on a cool day in the Veneto region of Italy. The gorgonzola adds a creaminess that contrasts nicely with the crunchy walnuts.

Toast the walnuts in a dry skillet over medium heat for 2 to 4 minutes until fragrant, then coarsely chop them.

Bring the stock to a simmer in a medium-size saucepan. Reduce the heat to keep the broth at a bare simmer.

Heat the olive oil over in a large skillet over medium-high heat. Add the onion, and season lightly with salt and pepper. Cook, stirring often, 3 to 5 minutes, or until the onion is translucent but not brown. Add the rice and cook, stirring, 2 to 4 minutes, or until the rice is lightly toasted.

Add the wine, then add enough of the hot broth to cover the rice. Cook, stirring occasionally, until the liquid is mostly absorbed. Keep adding broth to the pan ½ cup (120 ml) at a time and letting it absorb; repeat until the rice starts to turn tender, about 10 minutes total.

Stir in the chard. Continue adding the broth, letting it absorb each time, another 10 to 12 minutes, or until the rice is creamy but slightly firm to the tooth. (You may not need to use all the broth.)

Stir in three-fourths of the gorgonzola and three-fourths of the walnuts, and season to taste with salt and pepper. Serve the risotto topped with the remaining gorgonzola and walnuts.

YIELD: 2 TO 4 SERVINGS

½ cups (60 g) walnuts
4 cups (945 ml) chicken or vegetable stock
3 tablespoons (45 ml) olive oil
1 medium onion, diced
Salt and freshly ground black pepper
1½ cups (275 g) arborio or carnaroli rice
½ cup (120 ml) dry white wine
1 bunch chard, stemmed and thinly sliced
¾ cup (90 g) crumbled gorgonzola cheese

A creamy Italian rice dish, risotto is made by cooking short-grain rice varieties like arborio and carnaroli in wine and broth, which is added a little bit at a time until the liquid is absorbed. Risottos are made with a wide range of meat, seafood, and vegetables. Like pasta, risotto is usually served as a *primi*, or first course component of a traditional Italian meal.

☙ Saffron Chicken and Rice with Golden Beets ❧

Chicken and rice in one form or another is a classic combination the world over. It's the unofficial dish of Singapore and a favorite in Latin America and the Caribbean. The use of saffron and ginger is a nod to the likely Persian origin of the pilaf or pilau, and the beets are unconventional but go beautifully with the earthiness of the saffron.

Bring the water to a bare simmer. Season the chicken thighs generously all over with salt and pepper. In a small bowl, soak the saffron threads in ¼ cup (60 ml) of the hot water. Cut each beet into 8 pieces if using large beets, and into 6 pieces if using medium-size beets. Place the carrot, celery, shallot, garlic, and ginger in a food processor and purée.

Heat the olive oil over medium-high heat in a large, heavy skillet, and add the butter. When the butter stops foaming, add the chicken thighs, and brown well, 2 to 4 minutes per side. Remove the pan from the heat, and transfer the chicken to a plate.

Return the pan to the heat and add the puréed vegetables and the red pepper flakes, and cook, stirring often, 2 to 4 minutes, until fragrant. Add ½ cup (120 ml) of the hot water and scrape up the brown bits on the bottom of the pan. Add the rice and 1 teaspoon (6 g) kosher salt to the pan, and stir to coat.

Nestle the chicken thighs and beets into the rice mixture. Add the rest of the hot water and the saffron with its soaking liquid to the pan. Bring to a boil, reduce the heat, cover, and simmer 20 to 30 minutes, or until the chicken is cooked through. Add a little more water to the pan if it dries out before the chicken is done, or if too moist, turn up the heat at the end to evaporate any excess liquid. Remove the pan from the heat, and let stand, covered, for 10 minutes before serving.

YIELD: **2** TO **4** SERVINGS

2½ (570 ml) cups water

4 boneless, skinless chicken thighs

Kosher salt and black pepper

½ teaspoon saffron threads

3 large or medium golden beets, peeled

½ medium-size carrot, chopped

1 stalk celery, chopped

1 medium-size shallot, chopped

4 cloves garlic

1 piece ginger, 2-inches (5 cm) long, peeled and minced

2 teaspoons (10 ml) olive oil

1 tablespoon (14 g) unsalted butter

½ teaspoon red pepper flakes

1 cup (185 g) basmati rice

1 teaspoon (6 g) kosher salt

❧ Duck Breast with Pomegranate Glaze and Wild Rice ❧

Growing up we always had wild rice at Thanksgiving and Christmas, since its assertive texture and flavor went well with meat and game. Although the wild rice may seem an afterthought in this dish, it's an essential accompaniment to the duck and the sweet and sour glaze and sauce.

Cook the wild rice according to the package directions, and keep warm.

To make the glaze and sauce: Bring the chicken stock to a simmer over high heat, reduce to about ¼ cup (60 ml), and turn off the heat.

In a small saucepan over high heat, combine the pomegranate molasses and vinegar. Bring to a boil, then reduce to a simmer and stir in the honey. Simmer 10 to 15 minutes, or until the mixture has reduced by half. Transfer half of the glaze to the saucepan with the chicken stock, and stir to combine. Keep warm.

Preheat the oven to 350°F (180°C, or gas mark 4).

To make the duck: Heat the oil in a large ovenproof skillet over medium-high heat. Use a knife to lightly score the skin on the duck breasts in a crosshatch pattern without cutting all the way through the skin. Season both sides of the duck generously with salt and pepper. Place the duck skin side down in the hot skillet. (You may need to use 2 pans or do this in batches.) Cook 6 to 8 minutes, or until the skin is crisp. Turn the duck over, transfer the pan to the oven, and cook until desired doneness; an instant-read thermometer inserted in the thickest part should read 130°F (54°C) for medium-rare after 10 to 15 minutes.

Transfer the duck breasts to a plate, and brush them with the reserved ⅓ cup (115 g) glaze. Tent the duck loosely with aluminum foil, and let it rest 10 minutes.

Return the sauce to medium-low heat. Add the butter, and stir to combine. Cook 3 to 5 minutes, or until the sauce coats the back of a spoon. Season to taste with salt and pepper.

To serve: Slice the duck and place it on top of the rice; drizzle the sauce over all, and garnish with the fresh parsley leaves and the pomegranate seeds.

YIELD: **4 SERVINGS**

2 cups (320 g) wild rice

For the glaze and sauce:
2 cups (475 ml) chicken stock
⅔ cup (225 g) pomegranate molasses
⅔ cup (155 ml) red wine vinegar
¼ cup (85 g) honey

For the duck:
2 teaspoons canola or vegetable oil
4 boneless, skin-on duck breasts, about 7 ounces (200 g) each
Kosher salt and freshly ground black pepper
1 tablespoon (14 g) unsalted butter

Optional garnish:
½ cup fresh parsley leaves
½ cup (85 g) pomegranate seeds

❧ Forbidden Coconut Rice with Mango ❧

Rice makes its way into almost everything in Southeast Asia, even dessert. The combination of sweet rice, coconut milk, and mango is classic. Sticky white rice holds together more like a cake than the black rice does, but I like the depth of flavor of the black rice.

Combine the rice, water, and salt in a large, heavy pot; bring to a boil, cover, and cook about 30 minutes, or until the rice is tender. Drain the rice in a colander, rinse well with cold water, and let drain thoroughly.

In a large bowl, combine the rice, coconut cream, and honey. Refrigerate until chilled.

To serve top the rice with the mango and sprinkle with coconut, if desired.

YIELD: **6 TO 8 SERVINGS**

1½ cups (275 g) Chinese black forbidden rice

3 cups (710 ml) water

Pinch salt

1 cup (235 ml) coconut cream (the thick top part of canned coconut milk)

6 tablespoons (125 g) honey

3 to 4 mangoes, peeled and sliced

Optional garnish:

1 to 2 tablespoons (5 to 10 g) sweetened coconut

CORN

One summer in North Carolina, I planted a half-acre field of corn a few blocks from where I lived. Corn's sugars convert to starch fairly quickly, so freshly picked corn starts to deteriorate soon after picking. I wanted to taste corn before that happened. I watched over those stalks until the tassels formed and the husks were mature.

Once I started harvesting, I took my corn from farm to table in no time. I even had a few tastes of *huitlacoche*, the word used in Mexico for the prized noble fungus (with a truffle-like flavor) that appears on some of the ears.

Corn, or maize, is thought to have been domesticated in Mesoamerica close to ten thousand years ago. It spread throughout the Americas and then all over the world, where it's eaten in every conceivable way: fresh from the cob with butter in Alabama, with crumbled cotijo cheese and fresh thyme in Mexico, and as a sweet corn drink in Thailand. Polenta is a staple in Italy, where it's eaten like grits or allowed to harden and then cut and grilled, baked, or fried. In Lima, Peru, a variety of corn called *choclo*, which has very large kernels and a nutty flavor, is a traditional accompaniment to ceviche.

As the world's most consumed grain, corn has long been subjected to a curing process called *nixtamalization*, where it is soaked in an alkaline solution that releases essential nutrients in the corn, and turns it into hominy. When hominy is ground, the resulting meal is mixed with water to form a dough called *masa*, which is the essential dough for making tortillas. Cornmeal, corn flour, and polenta are usually made from nixtamalized corn—as is whole kernel hominy—which you can find canned or dried—and that adds a delicious nutty flavor to soups and stews.

I grew up in Alabama eating corn bread in dozens of different forms, from pones to cakes, and to this day, I can't think of anything better for eating with chili and other stews. Corn bread is especially good made with hot chiles, and I like to make it with different fats, too; including bacon fat and pork fat. Like many other quintessentially Southern ingredients, corn has a flavor affinity for tomatoes, onions, fresh herbs, and cheese.

You can season boiled or grilled corn on the cob with anything you can think of—a compound herb or spice butter, olive oil and Parmesan cheese, fresh thyme and minced garlic. Kernels are good scraped from the cob and simmered with heavy cream and butter to enrich the corn's inherent milkiness, and then tossed into salads, soups, stews, burritos, and tacos. One of my favorite simple salads in summer is fresh corn with tomatoes, cucumbers, marjoram or basil, and feta cheese, vinegar, and olive oil.

When you're choosing corn at the market, no matter the form, seek out interesting varieties. The darker colored the kernel, the more nutritious the corn. With fresh corn on the cob, check out the cut end of the cob to see how fresh it is. If it's green and fresh looking, then it was cut recently. If chalky or brown, it was cut a while ago and the quality won't be as good. And if you can, cook it cut straight off the stalk—you won't soon forget it.

☙ **Pickled Corn** ❧

If you've never had pickled corn before, this recipe is a revelation. When set aside for few days at room temperature, the corn ferments and develops tart flavors that enhance its sweetness. It's great on its own or used in cooking the same way you would use fresh corn, and is especially good in the pickled corn frittata also in this chapter.

2 quarts (2 L) water, divided

6 tablespoons (108 g) kosher salt, divided

6 ears fresh sweet corn, shucked, and cut through the cob into 1-inch (2.5 cm) pieces

2 medium-size shallots, sliced

6 Thai chiles, sliced

Bring 1 quart (1 L) of the water and 1 tablespoon (18 g) kosher salt to a boil in a large stockpot. Add the corn, stir, and return the water to a boil. Reduce to a simmer and cook for 2 minutes. Transfer the corn to a large bowl of ice water.

Stir together the remaining 1 quart (1 L) of water, 5 tablespoons (90 g) of salt, the shallots, and chiles in a large ceramic or glass container. Add the corn and cover the contents with a small plate or bowl to submerge the corn beneath the liquid.

Cover the container and set aside in a cool dark place for 1 to 3 days, tasting the corn periodically; the flavor will become more tart over time. When the corn tastes good to you, refrigerate it for up to 2 weeks submerged in the pickling liquid.

YIELD: 1 QUART (945 ml)

✤ Spinach and Pickled Corn Frittata ✤

I like frittatas as much on particularly hungry mornings as I do for a quick, inexpensive lunch or dinner alongside a simple salad. This version was inspired by the pickled corn recipe on the opposite page. The tang of the corn melds nicely with the egg and cream, and plenty of spinach balances out the richness and makes the meal more complete.

½ pound (225 g) fresh baby spinach

2 tablespoons (28 g) unsalted butter

1 cup (150 g) pickled corn

6 large eggs

3 tablespoons (45 ml) heavy cream

¼ teaspoon kosher salt

¼ teaspoon red pepper flakes

Preheat the oven to 300°F (150°C, or gas mark 2).

Heat a splash of water in a large oven-proof skillet over medium heat. Add the spinach and cook, stirring often, about 5 to 7 minutes, or until completely wilted and dark green. Drain the spinach in a colander, pressing out the excess liquid. Wrap the spinach in a kitchen towel and squeeze away any remaining liquid, then finely chop. Wipe out the skillet with paper towel.

Melt the butter in the same skillet over medium heat. In a large bowl, whisk together the spinach, corn, eggs, cream, salt, and pepper flakes. When the butter has melted, swirl to distribute it evenly in the pan. Add the spinach and egg mixture, transfer the skillet to the oven, and bake 15 to 20 minutes, or until the frittata is just set in the center.

YIELD: 2 TO 4 SERVINGS

❧ Grilled Oysters with Spicy, Sweet Corn Salsa ☙

Oysters and corn were likely some of the earliest native Southern foods, and this dish celebrates both. The smoky sweetness of the corn and the heat of the jalapeño dovetail beautifully with the briny oysters. I'm partial to the Apalachicola oysters I grew up eating, and also to the bold, briny oysters from the Lowcountry waters around Charleston.

If using a gas grill, heat it to medium. If using a charcoal grill, start the charcoal or wood briquettes; when the briquettes are ready, pile them on one side to make two zones, one for direct and one for indirect heat. The oysters will be cooked over the indirect side.

Heat the olive oil in a large skillet over medium-high heat, and toast the corn kernels for 2 to 4 minutes, or until they are browned and slightly blistered on both sides. Remove to a plate and let cool.

When the corn is cool, place it in a large bowl along with the tomato, red bell pepper, scallions, jalapeño, and cider vinegar and toss together; let marinate for 10 minutes.

In a sauté pan over medium heat, melt 5 tablespoons (70 g) of the butter. While the butter is foaming, add the marinated corn mixture and the salt, and heat through for 4 to 6 minutes, or until bubbly. Mix in the cilantro, and spoon over the oysters. Each oyster will take 1 to 3 teaspoons (5 to 16 g) of salsa, depending on its size.

Place the oysters on the grill over indirect heat, covered, for 5 to 10 minutes. The oysters are done when the edges have curled up and the topping is bubbly.

YIELD: 1 DOZEN OYSTERS

2 teaspoons (10 ml) olive oil

3 ears fresh sweet corn, kernels cut from the cob

1 large tomato, peeled, seeded, and diced

1 small red bell pepper, minced

3 scallions, thinly sliced

3/4 jalapeño chile, minced

3 tablespoons (45 ml) cider vinegar

5 tablespoons (70 g) unsalted butter, divided

1/2 teaspoon kosher salt

3 tablespoons (3 g) minced fresh cilantro

1 dozen oysters, shucked, shells reserved

❧ Corn, Tomato, Cucumber, and Feta Salad ❧

This simple salad is best made with the freshest ingredients from the summer garden. It's my go-to, basically uncooked summer salad, especially good alongside anything grilled. I like to stir the salad with the dressing until the feta breaks down just a little bit and coats of the vegetables.

Combine the corn, tomatoes, cucumbers, feta, and oregano in a large bowl. In a small bowl, whisk the vinegar, mustard, and a sprinkling of salt and pepper. Drizzle in the olive oil in a thin stream, whisking constantly until the dressing is emulsified. Add the vinaigrette to the salad a little at a time and toss until the dressing coats the vegetables, to taste.

YIELD: **4** TO **6** SERVINGS

4 cups (595 g) cooked sweet corn, (thawed and drained if frozen)

2 pints (about 50) cherry tomatoes, halved

2 medium-size cucumbers, peeled, seeded, and diced

8 ounces (225 g) feta, crumbled

2 tablespoons (8 g) chopped fresh oregano

2 tablespoons (30 ml) red wine vinegar

2 teaspoons (8 g) Dijon mustard

Salt and freshly ground black pepper

4 tablespoons (60 ml) olive oil

⌐ Spicy Shrimp Corn Fritters ⌐

Shrimp and corn are a natural match—the sweetness and earthiness of each bring out that quality of the other. These are much like the hushpuppies I grew up eating on the Florida panhandle. They were served at the only seafood restaurant—a dive about thirty minutes away—that served mostly fried seafood with tartar sauce, and three or four pies for dessert.

In a small sauté pan over medium heat, cook the diced red bell pepper and minced green onions in the olive oil until they are soft and fragrant, about 4 minutes. Transfer to a plate, stir in the lemon zest, and cool.

Add enough cooking oil to a heavy pot to come to a depth of 2 inches (5 cm), no more than halfway up the sides of the pan, and heat to 350°F (180°C). Combine the cornmeal, all-purpose flour, baking powder, sugar, sea salt, and cayenne pepper in a large bowl, and mix well.

In another bowl, whisk the buttermilk and the egg together. Add the dry ingredients to this mixture, and stir with a wooden spoon until combined. Fold in the sautéed red bell pepper and green onion mixture, and then the shrimp and the corn into the batter. Do not over mix or the batter will not be as light.

When the oil is up to temperature, drop the dough by rounded teaspoons into the hot oil. Fry them until puffed up and golden brown, turning once or twice, about 8 minutes. The fritters should be moist and cakelike on the inside and the shrimp cooked through. Remove the fritters from the oil with slotted spoon, drain on paper towels, and serve immediately.

YIELD: **3 DOZEN FRITTERS**

1/4 cup (38 g) finely diced red bell pepper

2 green onions, thinly sliced

2 teaspoons (10 ml) olive oil

1 teaspoon grated lemon zest

Vegetable, peanut, or canola oil, for frying

1 cup (140 g) cornmeal

1 cup (120 g) all-purpose flour

3 tablespoons (42 g) baking powder

1 tablespoon (13 g) sugar

1 teaspoon (6 g) fine sea salt

1/2 teaspoon cayenne pepper, or to taste

1/2 cup (120 ml) buttermilk

1 egg

1/2 pound (227 g) raw shrimp, peeled, deveined and diced

1 cup (150 g) cooked sweet corn (from approximately 2 ears)

❧ Pork, Hominy, and Squash Stew ❧

This dish is inspired by an Andean winter stew made with various cuts of pork, vegetables, and hominy, and garnished with cheese. It's a deeply satisfying and comforting version, with just enough chorizo added to enhance, but not dominate, the stew's flavor.

Season the pork all over with 1 teaspoon (6 g) of the salt. Set aside at room temperature for 20 to 30 minutes.

Pat the pork very dry with paper towels. Heat the oil in a large, heavy stockpot over medium-high heat. Add the pork and brown well on all sides, 6 to 8 minutes total. Transfer the pork to a plate.

Add the onion, habañero, chorizo, and dried thyme, and cook, breaking the sausage apart with a spoon, 2 to 4 minutes, or until the onion is translucent. Add the tomato purée and cook, stirring frequently, 4 to 6 minutes, or until the purée has thickened.

Add the bay leaves, 1 teaspoon (6 g) salt, water, and pork to the stockpot, bring to a boil, reduce to a moderate simmer, and cook about 45 minutes, or until the pork is starting to get tender. Add the hominy and squash, and cook, stirring occasionally, 30 to 45 minutes, or until the squash and pork are very tender. Remove and discard the bay leaves. To thicken the soup, transfer one-fourth of the squash to a food processor or bowl and purée or mash until smooth, then return the puréed squash to the stockpot.

Stir in the oregano and season to taste with salt. Serve with the cheese and avocado, if desired.

YIELD: **4** TO **6** SERVINGS

2 pounds (905 g) pork shoulder, excess fat trimmed away, cut into 1-inch (2.5 cm) pieces

2 teaspoons (12 g) kosher salt, divided, plus more to taste

1 tablespoon (15 ml) canola oil

1 yellow onion, diced

1 habañero chile, seeds and ribs removed for less heat, and diced

1 fresh chorizo sausage, casing removed

¼ teaspoon dried thyme

¾ cup (175 ml) tomato purée

2 bay leaves

8 cups (2 L) water, simmering

3 cups (495 g) cooked or canned hominy

1 medium-size butternut squash, peeled, and cut into 1-inch (2.5 cm) pieces

2 teaspoons (2.5 g) chopped fresh oregano

Optional garnishes:

Monterey Jack cheese, cubed

Diced avocado

❧ Cornmeal, Sausage, Shrimp, and Collard Green Soup ❧

Three classic dishes influence this soup: Brazil's *sopa de fuba*, Greece's *avgolemono*, and the South's shrimp and grits. It's a hearty soup that's substantial enough for a main course, and one that you could throw just about any leftovers into and it would be good. I like bratwurst here because it lets the natural corn flavor of the broth and the earthiness of the collards come through.

8 cups (1.9 L) chicken stock

½ cup (70 g) cornmeal

4 bratwurst sausages

1 pound (455 g) collard greens, stems removed and discarded, leaves cut into ½-inch (1.3 cm) squares

8 to 10 fresh shrimp, peeled and deveined

2 eggs

3 scallions, green parts only, thinly sliced

1 teaspoon (2 g) grated lemon zest

Kosher salt and freshly ground black pepper

Optional garnish:

1 tablespoon (3 g) minced chives

Preheat the oven to 350°F (180°C, or gas mark 4).

Bring the chicken stock to a boil in a large stockpot, and then reduce to a simmer. Toast the cornmeal in a medium-size, dry skillet over medium heat for 3 to 5 minutes until fragrant. Whisk the cornmeal into the chicken stock, stirring constantly to prevent lumping. Cook, stirring often, 20 to 30 minutes, or until mixture has thickened.

Meanwhile, place the sausages in a small casserole dish, and bake 20 to 25 minutes, or until cooked through and lightly browned. Cut the sausages into slices, and add them and the collard greens to the cornmeal and stock mixture. Simmer 15 to 20 minutes, or until the collards are very soft, then add the shrimp.

Put the eggs in a small bowl and whisk. Slowly drizzle 1 cup (235 ml) of the soup mixture into the eggs, stirring constantly, to temper the eggs so they don't scramble when added to the soup. Now pour the tempered egg mixture back into the stockpot, whisking constantly until incorporated. Immediately remove the pot from the heat. Stir in the scallions and lemon zest, season to taste with salt and pepper, and garnish with the chives, if desired.

YIELD: **4** TO **6** SERVINGS

ঽ **Sweet Potato Corn Bread** ও

This is one of my favorite takes on traditional corn bread. Sweet potato purée, when mixed in with cornmeal, adds a nice depth of flavor and nutritional integrity and a beautiful bright orange color. This is the base recipe, but the variations are endless: Try adding diced hot chiles, fresh herbs such as rosemary or chives, or grated aged cheese, or substituting sour cream or crème fraîche in place of the yogurt.

1 pound (455 g) orange-fleshed sweet potato (about 1 large)

Unsalted butter for preparing the baking pan

4 eggs

1 cup (235 ml) buttermilk

1 teaspoon (2 g) lemon zest

½ cup (115 g) full-fat plain yogurt

2⅓ cups (322 g) finely ground cornmeal

1 cup (125 g) all-purpose flour

1 tablespoon (11 g) baking powder

½ teaspoon baking soda

2 teaspoons (12 g) fine salt or table salt

2 teaspoons (9 g) granulated sugar

¼ teaspoon ground ginger

¼ teaspoon cayenne pepper

10 tablespoons (143 g) cold unsalted butter, diced

Preheat oven to 375°F (190°C, or gas mark 5). Pierce the sweet potato all over with a fork and bake directly on the middle rack of the oven for about 1 hour, or until tender all the way through. Alternatively, cook the sweet potato in a microwave on high, turning over once, about 10 minutes, or until tender. Let the sweet potato cool slightly, then peel and purée either with a potato ricer or masher. You'll need 1 cup (255 g) of purée.

Butter a 9 x 9 x 2-inch (23 x 23 x 5 cm), or similar size, baking pan. In a large bowl, whisk together the 1 cup (255 g) puréed sweet potatoes, eggs, buttermilk, yogurt, and lemon zest. Place the cornmeal, flour, baking powder, baking soda, salt, sugar, ginger, and cayenne pepper in a food processor, and pulse until combined. Add the butter to the food processor, and pulse until the mixture resembles coarse meal.

Add this cornmeal mixture to the sweet potato mixture, stir until just combined, and pour into the prepared baking pan. Bake 35 to 45 minutes, or until the corn bread is golden brown on top and a paring knife inserted into center comes out clean. Let cool slightly before serving.

YIELD: **10** TO **12** LARGE SLICES

SWEET POTATOES

On a trip last year to Vietnam, I spent a long day on a boat tour of the Mekong Delta. With a local guide, I sought out floating markets selling of all kinds of produce that thrive in the delta's tropical heat. At one of the markets, we climbed aboard a vendor's wooden boat and peered into the hold below, which was piled from floor to roof with sweet potatoes. We picked out a few of a variety that had a beautiful peach-colored interior flesh and took them with us to a local riverside restaurant, where the cooks incorporated them into a vegetable soup.

Sweet potatoes are a root vegetable related to morning glories. Like lots of quintessentially Southern vegetables, sweet potatoes thrive in warm, temperate climates all over the globe, and the vast majority of them are grown in Asia. They probably originated in Central or South America but were already being introduced to Japan and Korea as early as the mid-1700s, about the same time French settlers in the United States found Choctaws eating them as part of their native diet.

There are many more sweet potato varieties than just the common orange-fleshed type to which Americans are partial. They range in color from white to pale yellow to dark purple, with flavor and texture variations to match. What's common to them all, of course, is that they're sweeter than potatoes. I try to cook with as many different varieties as I can get my hands on, favoring the more subtle lighter-fleshed varieties for savory preparations and orange-fleshed varieties for sweet dishes.

I'm partial to simplicity in cooking, and that's especially true with sweet potatoes. My favorite way to eat them is simply rubbed with good quality olive oil and coarse sea salt and baked until their skins are crisp and their flesh tender and sweet. They're great that way as a side dish or, drizzled with a little honey and topped with crumbled toasted nuts, as a breakfast food. I also love the way sweet potatoes are treated in Japan: lightly fried tempura-style to lock in their flavor; boiled and paired with a soy-based sauce; or steamed and tossed with a ginger-miso dressing.

In Brazil and the Caribbean, sweet potatoes are a nutritional workhorse, incorporated into rustic stews, often with rich, flavorful cuts of beef and pork. In Peru, they're simply boiled and traditionally served as a garnish for the area's legendary ceviches. In the Middle East, they're roasted and added to colorful salads. I also like to use sweet potatoes rather than potatoes for rich gratins and gnocchi.

At the market, look for sweet potatoes without blemishes or bruises. They should be smooth skinned, feel firm and heavy for their size, and look like they've been handled carefully. I usually peel them before incorporating them into soups and stews, but the skin is good for you and tastes good, too, so I like to keep the skin if possible.

❧ Roasted Sweet Potatoes with Tahini Yogurt ❧

This dish is inspired by a recipe in Claudia Roden's classic cookbook, *Arabesque*. Sweet potatoes are common in Mediterranean countries, such as Turkey, Lebanon, and Morocco. The combination here of pomegranate molasses (or honey) and lemon juice gives them a sweet and sour taste, and the nutty tahini yogurt mixture complements their earthiness.

Preheat the oven to 425°F (220°C, or gas mark 7). Brush the sweet potato wedges lightly with olive oil, and roast them on a baking sheet for 30 to 40 minutes, or until tender and brown in spots.

In a small bowl, whisk together the pomegranate molasses, lemon juice, cayenne pepper, and 2 tablespoons (28 ml) olive oil. In a separate bowl, whisk together the yogurt, garlic, and tahini.

When the sweet potatoes are done, brush them generously with the molasses mixture and transfer them to a serving platter. Drizzle the tahini yogurt over the sweet potatoes, and then sprinkle with the pomegranate seeds, mint, and sesame seeds, if desired.

YIELD: **4** TO **6** SERVINGS

2 pounds (905 g) sweet potatoes (about 3 medium), unpeeled and cut into about 24 wedges

2 tablespoons (28 ml) olive oil, plus more for brushing the sweet potatoes

1 tablespoon (20 g) pomegranate molasses (or honey)

1½ tablespoon (7 ml) fresh lemon juice

Pinch cayenne pepper

1 cup (230 g) low-fat plain yogurt

1 clove garlic, minced

2 tablespoons (30 g) tahini

½ cup (85 g) pomegranate seeds

Optional garnishes:
Fresh mint leaves
Sesame seeds

❧ **Peruvian-Style Flounder Ceviche** ❧

Peruvians are famous for—and fanatical about—ceviche, and sweet potatoes and corn are surprisingly good traditional accompaniments. During a recent trip to Lima, I tried ceviche all kinds of ways both in dives and in upscale restaurants. This simple version is my favorite. It's all about the balance of impeccably fresh fish, acidity, and the *leche de tigre*, or "tiger's milk," that holds it all together as a kind of sea-infused sauce. (Leche de tigre is often made with fish broth, but I like the simpler version below.)

1 pound (455 g) sweet potato (about 1 large)

2 ears fresh sweet corn

¼ red onion, thinly sliced, divided

2 pounds (905 g) flounder fillet, trimmed to make square edges, scraps reserved

½ cup (120 ml) freshly squeezed lime juice

½ teaspoon grated fresh ginger

1 clove garlic, minced

1 stalk celery, peeled and thinly sliced

3 aji limo chiles or 1 habañero chile with seeds and ribs removed for less heat, thinly sliced, divided

2 teaspoons (12 g) kosher salt, plus more to taste

1 cup (16 g) sliced fresh cilantro leaves

Bring a large saucepan of water to a boil, add the sweet potato, turn down the heat, and gently simmer 30 to 45 minutes, or until just cooked through but still slightly firm. A few minutes before the sweet potato is done, add the corn and simmer 5 to 7 minutes, or until cooked through. Remove the ears, cool, and cut the corn from the cob. Cool, peel, and slice the sweet potato. To mellow the flavor of the sliced onions, soak them in a bowl of ice water for 10 minutes, then drain.

To make the leche de tigre, place the flounder scraps in a large glass bowl along with the lime juice, half of the red onion slices, the ginger, garlic, and celery, and two-thirds of the sliced chiles. Set this mixture aside for 20 to 30 minutes, then pass through a fine-mesh strainer into a bowl, pressing firmly on the fish, onion, and aromatics to release their flavorful liquid, then discard everything but the strained liquid. Season to taste with salt.

To prepare the fish for the ceviche, cut the squared off flounder pieces into even strips, 2 to 4 inches (5 to 10 cm) long and ¼-inch (6 mm) thick. Cut these strips in half, and place them in a medium-size glass bowl set in a larger bowl filled with ice. This will keep the fish cold. Sprinkle the fish with the 2 teaspoons (16 g) kosher salt, and stir several times to coat evenly. Let this mixture sit for 20 minutes, gently stirring every few minutes so the salt will penetrate and season the fish.

Add the remaining one-third sliced chile, the remaining one-half red onion, and the cilantro to the fish, and stir to combine. Slowly add the leche de tigre, stirring several times. Pour the ceviche into a serving bowl, and serve with the sweet potato slices, and a mound of the corn on the side.

YIELD: **4** TO **6** SERVINGS

❧ Sweet Potato Gnocchi with Gorgonzola Sauce ☙

Using sweet potatoes rather than regular potatoes when making gnocchi lends a Southern bent to this classic Italian dumpling dish. The assertive flavor and creaminess of the gorgonzola is a particularly good match with the sweet potatoes.

Preheat oven to 375°F (190°C, or gas mark 5). Pierce the sweet potatoes all over with a fork and bake directly on the middle rack of the oven for about 1 hour, or until tender all the way through. Alternatively, cook the sweet potatoes in a microwave on high, turning over once, about 10 minutes, or until tender.

Peel the sweet potatoes, and mash them in a large bowl. Add the salt, eggs, and then add the flour a little at a time, stirring to combine; stir the mixture about 1 minute, or until the dough just comes together. Be careful not to overwork the dough or the gnocchi will be tough. The dough should be slightly sticky, so you may need a little more or a little less flour to get the right consistency.

Transfer the dough to a lightly floured work surface, and divide into quarters. Form each quarter into a ball, then roll each ball into a long dowel shape, continuing to lightly dust with flour as needed to prevent sticking. Cut each dowel into 1-inch (2.5 cm) pieces, and then roll each piece against the tines of a fork to create ridges in the gnocchi.

Bring a large saucepan of salted water to a boil. Meanwhile, combine the milk and gorgonzola in a large skillet, and cook over medium heat until sauce consistency. Cook the gnocchi in the boiling water, adjusting the heat so the boil is gentle, stirring once or twice, 6 to 8 minutes, or until the gnocchi float and are cooked through. Transfer the gnocchi to the skillet with the sauce, and cook 1 to 2 minutes, stirring to coat the gnocchi with the sauce. Stir in the chives, and season to taste with black pepper.

YIELD: **4** TO **6** SERVINGS

2 pounds (905 g) sweet potatoes (about 2 large)

½ teaspoon kosher salt

2 eggs, whisked

2 to 3 cups (250 to 375 g) all-purpose flour

½ cup (120 ml) whole milk

6 ounces (170 g) gorgonzola cheese

2 tablespoons (6 g) minced fresh chives

Freshly ground black pepper

🥒 Gnocchi are an Italian pasta-like dish of soft dumplings, which are boiled and then served with a sauce. Their makeup varies by region, usually some combination of wheat flour and eggs, potatoes, spinach, ricotta and Parmesan cheeses. Before boiling, the formed dumplings are often imprinted with the back of a fork to create ridges that hold on to sauce.

❧ Sweet Potato Salad with Miso Dressing ❧

I love the way the Japanese treat sweet potatoes—simply fried, steamed, or boiled, and topped with an assertively flavorful sauce. Miso, or fermented soybean paste, is a natural match with sweet potatoes. I think of this dish as a Japanese-inspired take on potato salad—great as a simple lunch on its own, or as summer picnic side dish with barbecue.

2 pounds (905 g) sweet potatoes (about 2 large), peeled and cut into 1-inch (2.5 cm) pieces

4 tablespoons (48 g) white miso

4 tablespoons (60 ml) mirin

1 teaspoon (2 g) freshly grated lemon zest

Cayenne pepper

Optional garnish:

2 scallions, green parts only, thinly sliced

Steam the sweet potato pieces in a steamer basket inserted into a saucepan, or in a bamboo steamer, for 15 to 20 minutes, or until tender but not mushy. Transfer to a platter to cool.

In a large bowl, whisk together the miso and mirin. When the sweet potatoes are still warm or at room temperature, gently toss them with the miso dressing, lemon zest, and season to taste with cayenne pepper. Sprinkle with the scallion, if desired

YIELD: 4 TO 6 SERVINGS

101

❧ Sweet Potato Gratin ❧

I started making gratins when I lived in Paris, guided by Patricia Wells's cookbooks, and using the beautiful potatoes and dairy available in local markets. Sweet potatoes pair beautifully with cream, and this classic gratin is a case in point. I like it as a go-to Thanksgiving or Christmas side, or as an early fall accompaniment to a pork roast. Don't use white-fleshed sweet potatoes for this dish, as their flesh tends to discolor once they're sliced.

1 cup (235 ml) heavy cream

1 bay leaf

1 piece fresh ginger, 2 to 3 inches (5 to 7.5 cm) long, peeled and thinly sliced

3 whole sage leaves, lightly bruised

Pinch cayenne pepper

1/2 teaspoon kosher salt

1 pound (455 g) sweet potatoes, peeled and sliced into 1/8-inch (3 mm) thick pieces

Preheat the oven to 375°F (190°C, or gas mark 5). Combine the cream, bay leaf, ginger, sage, pepper, and salt in a small saucepan and bring to a simmer over medium-high heat. Simmer for 1 minute, then remove from the heat and let steep 10 minutes. Remove the bay leaf, ginger, and sage leaves, reserving the sage leaves for topping the gratin.

Pour one-third of the cream into the bottom of a medium-size baking dish. (I like a deep one, which gives you more layers. My favorite is a roughly 10 x 7-inch, or 25 x 18 cm, oval baking dish). Arrange half the sweet potato slices, overlapping each slice by about half, on top of the cream. Then top with another one-third of the cream. Repeat this one more time, topping with the remaining one-third of the cream. Place the sage leaves on top of the gratin. Cover with foil, and bake for 30 minutes.

Remove the foil and gently press the sweet potatoes down to submerge them in the cream. Bake another 15 to 20 minutes, uncovered, or until the sweet potatoes are tender and the cream browned and bubbly.

YIELD: **4** SERVINGS

❧ Chicken, Sweet Potato, and Corn Stew ❧

This dish is inspired by a New World *cocido*, or Spanish stew, and made with chicken, sweet potatoes, and corn. You could easily substitute stewing beef, pork, or fresh or cured sausages, and any vegetable you have on hand.

Soak the chickpeas in water overnight, then drain, and rinse well. Season the chicken thighs generously on both sides with salt and pepper, and set aside for 30 minutes.

Bring 2½ quarts, (10 cups, or 2.5 L), water to a boil. Meanwhile, pat the chicken thighs dry. Heat the canola oil in a large, heavy stockpot over medium-high heat. Cook the chicken, turning once, about 6 minutes, or until brown on both sides. Add the onion, carrot, celery, and jalapeño, and cook, stirring once or twice, 2 minutes.

Add the hot water, chickpeas, and bouquet garni, and bring to a boil. Reduce to a simmer and cook, stirring occasionally, 1 to 1½ hours, or until the chickpeas are almost tender. Skim off any foam that rises to the surface and add more water to cover if necessary.

Remove the chicken thighs and set them aside to cool slightly. Add the cabbage, corn, and sweet potatoes, and 1 teaspoon (6 g) of salt to the pot. Bring to a boil, reduce to a simmer, and cook 15 to 20 minutes, or until the vegetables are tender.

Remove and discard the bouquet garni. Cut the chicken off the bone and into bite-size pieces, and return the meat to the pot. Stir in the cilantro, and season to taste with salt and pepper. Serve with lime wedges, if desired.

YIELD: **4 TO 6 SERVINGS**

1 cup (200 g) dried chickpeas

6 skinless, bone-in chicken thighs

Salt and freshly ground black pepper

1 tablespoon (15 ml) canola oil

1 medium-size yellow onion, chopped

1 carrot, peeled and chopped

1 stalk celery, chopped

1 jalapeño pepper, sliced (optional)

1 bouquet garni (3 peppercorns, 4 cloves garlic, 6 to 8 cilantro stems, 1 bay leaf, and 4 sprigs thyme enclosed in a piece of cheesecloth and secured with a piece of kitchen twine)

1 medium-size head savoy cabbage, chopped

1 ear fresh sweet corn, cut into 2-inch (2.5 cm) rounds

1 pound (455 g) sweet potato (about 1 large), peeled and cut into 2-inch (2.5 cm) pieces

1 teaspoon (6 g) kosher salt, or more to taste

1 cup (16 g) fresh cilantro leaves

Optional garnish:

Fresh lime wedges

🌶 *Cocido* is a Spanish stew made with chickpeas, a variety of fresh and cured meats, and vegetables such as potatoes, carrots, cabbage, and turnips. Common to Madrid, cocido traveled with the Spaniards to Mexico and Central and South America, where it was incorporated with the local native vegetables there.

Sweet Potato Apple Crisp

In this dessert, sweet potatoes take on a luxurious sweetness made a little exotic by the addition of garam masala. The apples lend the filling a tart counterpoint, and the pecans add buttery nuttiness to the topping. You'll need patience (and maybe two large skillets) to make the filling, but the results make it worth the effort.

To make the crust: Preheat the oven to 375°F (190°C, or gas mark 5). Line a 13 x 9 x 2-inch (33 x 23 x 5 cm) baking pan with parchment paper. In the bowl of a stand mixer fitted with the paddle attachment (or using an electric hand-held mixer), cream together the butter and sugar at medium speed about 2 minutes, or until fluffy. Reduce the speed to low, and add the flour and salt. Mix about 1 minute, or until a uniform soft dough forms. Form the dough into a ball, and then press it evenly into the bottom of the sheet pan. Bake on the center rack of the oven about 20 minutes, or until golden brown. Set aside to cool.

To make the filling: Slice the sweet potatoes and apples as thinly as possible with a mandolin or sharp knife. In a large skillet (or 2 large skillets if necessary) over medium-high heat, melt the butter and brown sugar. Add the sweet potatoes and apples, increase the heat to high, and cook, stirring and turning often, 10 min-

utes, or until softened. Stir in the garam masala, reduce the heat to medium-high. Adding the water a little bit at a time as necessary to prevent scorching, cook another 10 minutes, or until the mixture is tender and caramelized. Set aside.

To make the topping: Toast the pecans in a sheet pan in the preheated oven about 10 minutes, or until they turn a shade darker. Let cool, and coarsely chop. In a large bowl, combine the pecans, oats, flour, sugar, garam masala, baking soda, and salt, and stir to combine. Add the butter, and working quickly with your fingers, cut the butter into the flour mixture until evenly incorporated and crumbly.

To assemble: Spread the filling evenly onto the crust. Pour the topping over the filling and press to distribute evenly. Bake in the 375°F (190°C, or gas mark 5) oven, rotating the pan once, for 18 to 20 minutes, or until golden brown.

YIELD: **8 TO 12 BARS**

For the crust:

4 tablespoons (55 g) unsalted butter, at room temperature

1/3 cup (65 g) granulated sugar

1 1/2 cups (62 g) all-purpose flour

1/4 teaspoon kosher salt

For the filling:

1 1/2 pounds (680 g) sweet potatoes, peeled

4 Granny Smith apples (about 1 pound, or 455 g)

3 tablespoons (42 g) unsalted butter

1/4 cup (60 g) packed light brown sugar

1 teaspoon (2 g) garam masala or cinnamon

1 cup (235 ml) water, or less as needed

For the topping:

1/2 cup (100 g) whole pecans

1 3/4 cups (140 g) quick-cooking oats

1 3/4 cups (220 g) all-purpose flour

3/4 cup (170 g) packed light brown sugar

1 teaspoon (2 g) garam masala

1/4 teaspoon baking soda

1/4 teaspoon kosher salt

3/4 cup (167 g) unsalted butter, chilled, and cut into 1 1/2-inch (3.8 cm) pieces

❧ Sweet Potato, Sorghum, and Rum Flan ❧

This is a dessert I imagine showing up on a Barbadian sugarcane planter's table. Sugarcane production on islands such as Barbados was one of the first big draws for English settlers to the New World, and rum production soon followed. Many of the first planters to land in Lowcountry South Carolina came from Barbados looking for new opportunities. Sorghum syrup gives this flan additional Southern flavor.

For the caramel:

2 cups (400 g) granulated sugar
½ cup (120 ml) water

For the flan:

1 pound (455 g) sweet potato (about 1 large)
1 cup (235 ml) milk, divided
1 cup (235 ml) heavy cream, divided
6 tablespoons (72 g) granulated sugar
⅔ cup (155 ml) water
1 cup (235 ml) sweetened condensed milk
2 teaspoons (10 ml) vanilla extract
1 tablespoon (15 ml) dark rum
2 tablespoons (30 ml) sorghum syrup
5 large eggs
2 egg yolks

To make the caramel: Combine the sugar and water in a medium-size saucepan, and cook over low heat, without stirring, about 5 minutes, or until the syrup turns amber; brush the sides of the pan with a pastry brush dipped in water as needed to prevent sugar crystals from forming. Pour the caramel into 6 small (1 cup, or 235 ml) ramekins, and tilt to evenly coat the bottom and a little bit up the sides. Set aside.

To make the flan: Preheat oven to 375°F (190°C, or gas mark 5). Pierce the sweet potato all over with a fork and bake directly on the middle rack of the oven for about 1 hour, or until tender all the way through. Alternatively, cook the sweet potato in a microwave on high, turning over once, about 10 minutes, or until tender. Peel, cut into pieces, and purée the sweet potato in a food processor. With the machine running, add ½ cup (120 ml) of the milk and ½ cup (120 ml) of the cream, and process until smooth.

In a large bowl, combine the sugar, the remaining ½ cup (120 ml) of cream and ½ cup (120 ml) of milk, the water, sweetened condensed milk, vanilla extract, rum, and sorghum syrup. Mix well.

Preheat the oven to 325°F (170°C, or gas mark 3).

In another large bowl, whisk together the eggs and egg yolks until smooth. Pour the eggs into the cream and rum mixture, and whisk to combine. Add the sweet potato mixture and stir to combine. Divide this mixture evenly among the ramekins. Place the ramekins in a large deep roasting pan, and add enough hot water to come halfway up the sides of the ramekins. Bake for 2 hours, or until the custard is mostly set, but the center but still a little jiggly. Remove from the oven, and transfer the flans to a rack to cool.

When cool, refrigerate the flans until cold, at least 4 hours, or overnight. To unmold, run a thin knife around the sides of the ramekins, cover each ramekin with a plate, and invert.

YIELD: **6** SERVINGS

LIMA BEANS

On a typical school night when I was growing up, my mom would cook us lima beans simply sautéed with butter and salt and pepper, or mixed together with fresh corn for succotash. As is typical in the South, we called limas "butterbeans," and to this day the smell of them simmering in the kitchen makes me nostalgic for the kind of everyday Southern home cooking I grew up on.

Limas are nutritional, versatile, and easy to prepare. Their earthy flavor and creamy texture means they go especially well with assertive tomatoes, woodsy herbs such as thyme and rosemary, pork and chicken, citrus and vinegar, chiles, and all kinds of cheeses. For inspiration, especially in summer when I have loads of limas on hand, I look to other beans and legumes, and to the cuisines and dishes that use them.

Take fava beans, for example. They're incorporated into dishes from all over the world, especially in Mediterranean countries. They aren't as commonly used in the tropical heat and humidity of the South. Limas are similar to favas in shape, color, and flavor, so I work limas into a bruschetta dish or a spring ragout in the same way cooks would use favas in Italy or France. Limas work well as a substitute for chickpeas, too, as in an otherwise classic hummus. They're also at home in a traditional Peruvian *solterito* salad or in a burrito in place of black beans or pintos.

Lima beans are a New World legume that likely originated in the Andes. As the name suggests, Europeans around Lima, Peru, discovered them. Varieties such as the large white, baby white, Christmas, Hopi orange, and red offer a diverse range of flavors and textures. Christmas limas have a firm texture and chestnut-like flavor that pairs especially well with aggressive seasonings. Large white limas are good for soups since their creamy texture and soft skins purée well. The green and speckled varieties are abundant in Charleston's summer farmers' markets, and those are the ones I cook with the most.

Limas are freshly shelled and abundant in summer in the South and are available frozen and dried all year round. Dried limas should be soaked like other beans and take longer to cook than fresh ones, an hour or so depending on their size. Waiting to add salt toward the end of cooking is a good way to ensure that limas turn tender. A well-flavored lima bean broth is delicious just on its own or as a soup with the limas puréed right in it. I keep cooked limas in the fridge, either immersed in their cooking liquid or drained and tossed with a little vinegar, so I can keep cooking with them for several days after I make a batch.

◦ Baked Lima Beans ◦

The earthy flavors of lima beans stand up well in this classic American bean dish. This one's especially good in summer when limas and fresh tomatoes are in season. Let the limas bubble away in the oven, or cook them in an ovenproof dish right on the grill for a smokier flavor. The paprika adds smoke flavor, too.

Preheat the oven to 400°F (200°C, or gas mark 6).

Cook the bacon in the canola oil in a large saucepan over medium-high heat, stirring often, 2 to 4 minutes, or until the bacon starts to turn crisp and brown a little. Add the onion, red pepper flakes, and smoked paprika, and cook, stirring often, 2 to 4 minutes, or until the onions are translucent. Add the garlic and tomato paste, and cook, stirring constantly, about 30 seconds. Add the apple cider vinegar, soy sauce, mustard, sugar, and tomatoes, and bring to a boil. Fold in the lima beans and sage, then add up to 1½ cups (355 ml) or just enough water to make the mixture pourable, but not so much that it's soupy. Bring to a simmer, then pour the mixture into an 8-inch (20 cm) round earthenware casserole dish. Bake 45 to 60 minutes, or until hot and bubbly.

YIELD: 4 TO 6 SERVINGS

8 slices thick-cut bacon, diced

2 teaspoons (10 ml) canola oil

1 onion, diced

2 teaspoons (2.4 g) dried red pepper flakes (optional)

1 teaspoon (2.5 g) smoked paprika

6 cloves garlic, minced

2 tablespoons (32 g) tomato paste

4 tablespoons (60 ml) apple cider vinegar

2 tablespoons (30 ml) soy sauce

2 tablespoons (22 g) Dijon mustard

½ cup (115 g) packed light brown sugar

2 cups (360 g) diced tomatoes

4 cups (680 g) cooked lima beans

4 tablespoons (10 g) minced fresh sage

1½ cups (355 ml) water, or less as needed

❧ Butterbean Hummus ☙

I'll never forget exploring the various hummus restaurants in Jerusalem and Tel Aviv, where it's often eaten for breakfast, and where disputes over the best hummus spots reach biblical proportions. Back home in the South, lima beans are a fresh substitute for the chickpeas called for in classic hummus. Baby limas are probably the closest to chickpeas in color and flavor, but any lima variety will work here. Hummus is all about personal taste and balance, so try different amounts of limas, tahini, lemon juice, and garlic.

4 tablespoons (60 g) sesame tahini

Juice of 1 lemon, or to taste, divided

1 clove garlic, minced, divided

2½ cups (425 g) cooked lima beans

1 tablespoon (15 g) nonfat Greek yogurt

1 tablespoon (15 ml) lima bean cooking liquid or water

Kosher salt

Optional garnish:

Olive oil, for drizzling

In a small bowl, mix together the tahini with one-half of the lemon juice and one-half of the garlic to lighten the tahini's texture. Combine the tahini mixture, the remaining lemon juice, garlic, lima beans, yogurt, and lima bean cooking liquid in a food processor, and blend until smooth. Season to taste with salt, and then blend again to incorporate the salt. Drizzle with olive oil, if desired.

YIELD: 2 TO 3 CUPS (490 TO 740 G)

⊰ **Solterito Salad** ⊱

The name of this classic Peruvian salad means "single man," probably because it's easy to put together and nutritionally diverse, both good attributes for a simple meal. It's also reminiscent of the classic Greek salad you'll find in just about every casual restaurant in Athens and throughout the Greek islands. Feta cheese makes a good substitute for the queso fresco here.

Combine the onion, serrano, and vinegar in a large bowl, and set aside for 10 to 20 minutes. This will mellow the red onion's flavor and bring out the chile's heat. Add the lima beans, corn, tomatoes, cheese, olives, and parsley, and toss to combine; season to taste with salt and pepper.

YIELD: **4** TO **6** SERVINGS

½ medium-size red onion, diced

1 serrano chile, ribs and seeds removed for less heat, diced

3 tablespoons (45 ml) red wine vinegar

2 cups (340 g) cooked lima beans

1 cup (150 g) cooked sweet corn

12 cherry tomatoes, halved

1¼ cups (190 g) diced queso fresco cheese

½ cup good-quality pitted black olives

2 tablespoons (8 g) chopped fresh parsley

Kosher salt and freshly ground black pepper

ᣔ Butterbean Bruschetta with Parmesan and Basil ᣚ

Although smaller lima beans more closely resemble fava or white beans—both used in bruschettas in Italy—I like the bold flavor of Christmas limas in this dish. No matter the bean, bruschettas are about good bread, simple toppings, and generosity with good-quality olive oil.

4 cloves garlic, peeled

4 large, thick slices good-quality rustic Italian or French bread

6 tablespoons (90 ml) olive oil

1 serrano chile, seeds and ribs removed for less heat, thinly sliced

12 cherry tomatoes, halved

3 cups (510 g) cooked lima beans

4 to 6 fresh basil leaves, torn

Parmesan cheese

Thinly slice two of the garlic cloves. Toast or grill the bread until crisp on the outside but still tender on the inside. Rub each slice of bread briskly with one clove of the peeled garlic to flavor it.

Heat the olive oil in a large skillet over medium heat. Add the sliced garlic and serrano chile, and cook, stirring often to coat the garlic with the oil, 2 to 4 minutes, or until the garlic is fragrant and starting to change color. Add the tomatoes and lima beans, and increase the heat to medium high. Cook, stirring often, until the limas and tomatoes are hot and flavored with the garlic, chile, and oil. Stir in the basil leaves. Spoon the lima beans and tomatoes over the bread, and top to taste with freshly grated Parmesan cheese.

YIELD: 4 SERVINGS

❧ Lima Bean and Potato Soup ❧

The comforting combination of limas and potatoes most likely originated in the Andes, where many varieties of potatoes were grown centuries ago. Any lima variety would work here, but the large white variety purées especially well. This is a meatless version, but a handful of diced thick-cut bacon pieces sautéed with the olive oil and leeks would make for a more decadent soup.

2 tablespoons (30 ml) olive oil

2 leeks, white and pale green parts only, thinly sliced

Salt and white pepper

2 pounds (905 g) russet potatoes, peeled and cut into 2-inch (5 cm) pieces

4 cups (680 g) cooked lima beans, preferably large white limas

2 cups (475 ml) lima bean cooking liquid or chicken stock

Heat the olive oil in a large saucepan over medium-high heat. Add the leeks and a light sprinkling of salt, and cook, stirring often, 2 minutes. Add the potatoes, lima beans, and lima bean cooking liquid or chicken stock. Add enough water to cover, bring to a boil, reduce to a simmer, and cook about 30 minutes, or until the potatoes are very tender and the lima beans begin to fall apart. You may need to add a little water if the soup gets too dry. Season to taste with salt and white pepper.

YIELD: **4** TO **6** SERVINGS

⤳ Three Sisters Succotash ⤳

Succotash is a traditional Southern dish inspired by the Native American "three sisters"—corn, beans, and squash—grown together in hot climates for both practical and nutritional reasons. The beans infused the soil with nitrogen to help the squash grow, the corn stalk supported the climbing bean, and the leaves of the squash plant were a living mulch that kept moisture in and weeds out. When they are eaten together, the protein is more complete, and the sweetness of the corn enhances the flavor of the limas and squash.

2 tablespoons (30 ml) olive oil

2 tablespoons (28 g) unsalted butter

1 medium yellow onion, diced

1 pound (455 g) yellow squash, cut into 2-inch (5 cm) pieces

3 cups (510 g) cooked lima beans

2 cups (300 g) sweet corn

2 teaspoons (1.7 g) finely chopped marjoram or basil

1 cup (235 ml) chicken stock or lima bean cooking liquid

2 teaspoons (10 ml) rice wine vinegar

Salt and pepper

Melt the olive oil and butter together in a large saucepan over medium-high heat. Add the onion and cook, stirring often, 2 to 4 minutes, or until translucent. Add the squash, reduce the heat to medium, cover, and cook, stirring occasionally, 6 to 8 minutes, or until the squash softens slightly. Add the lima beans, corn, marjoram or basil, and chicken stock or cooking liquid, and cook, stirring often, 4 to 6 minutes, or until the squash is tender but not falling apart. Stir in the vinegar, season to taste with salt and pepper.

YIELD: **4** TO **6** SERVINGS

❧ Fusilli with Lima Beans, Pecans, Ricotta, and Basil ❧

This is one of those simple dishes that are easy to put together without a trip to the store if you have a few basic fridge and pantry staples on hand. I often go for whole-wheat pasta and substitute cottage cheese if I don't have ricotta. Lemon zest balances the cheese with bright citrus flavor, and pecans or walnuts add crunch and protein.

1 pound (455 g) fusilli pasta

Kosher salt

2 cups (340 g) cooked lima beans

2 cups (200 g) pecans

2 cups (500 g) part-skim ricotta cheese

2 tablespoons (30 ml) olive oil

2 teaspoons (8 g) lemon zest

4 to 6 basil leaves, torn into pieces

Freshly ground black pepper

Cook the pasta in generously salted water until al dente. Just before the pasta is done, stir in the lima beans to warm them through. Drain, reserving 1 cup (235 ml) of the pasta cooking liquid. Toast the pecans in a small, dry skillet over medium heat about 2 minutes, or until lightly browned and fragrant. Coarsely grind them in a food processor or with a mortar and pestle.

In a large bowl, combine the ricotta, pecans, olive oil, lemon zest, and basil. Add the cooked pasta to this mixture, and stir to combine, adding as much of the reserved warm pasta water as needed so the sauce coats the pasta. Season to taste with freshly ground black pepper.

YIELD: **4 SERVINGS**

Chicken, Lima Bean, Asparagus, and Mushroom Ragout

The combination of chicken, cream, tarragon, and lemon in this dish is classic and elegant, and the lima beans add earthiness. It's great on its own or alongside egg noodles lightly dressed in olive oil.

Season the chicken pieces all over with salt and pepper, and set aside at room temperature for up to 20 minutes.

Melt the butter and olive oil together in a large skillet over medium-high heat. Add the onion and cook, stirring often, 2 to 4 minutes, or until it starts to turn translucent. Add the chicken and cook, turning once or twice and stirring the onions, 2 to 4 minutes, or until the chicken is lightly browned on all sides. Lower the heat slightly if the onions start to brown.

Add the mushrooms, asparagus, and chicken stock. Bring to a boil, reduce to a simmer, and cook, stirring often, 4 to 6 minutes, or until the asparagus start to turn bright green. Add the tomatoes, lima beans, and cream, and cook 2 to 4 minutes, or until the sauce thickens and the asparagus are just tender.

When the chicken is just cooked through, turn off the heat, and stir in the tarragon and lemon zest. Season to taste with salt and white pepper.

YIELD: **4** TO **6** SERVINGS

- 2 boneless, skinless chicken breast halves, cut into 2-inch (5 cm) pieces
- Kosher salt and freshly ground white pepper
- 2 tablespoons (28 g) unsalted butter
- 1 tablespoon (15 ml) olive oil
- 1 yellow onion, diced
- 8 ounces (225 g) mixed oyster, shiitake, or other fresh mushrooms, sliced
- 8 ounces (225 g) asparagus, sliced on the bias (about 3 cups)
- 1 cup (235 ml) chicken stock
- 12 cherry tomatoes, halved
- 1½ cups (255 g) cooked lima beans
- ½ cup (120 ml) heavy cream
- 2 teaspoons (2.6 g) chopped tarragon
- 2 teaspoons (4 g) lemon zest

A ragout is a dish made with bite-size pieces of lean meat cooked relatively quickly (unlike a stew, which cooks for a long time to break down the meat), along with aromatics, vegetables, and a surrounding sauce.

PEANUTS

The first time I tasted peanuts outside of the South was on a safari in Tanzania. On the rim of the Ngorongoro Crater, in a makeshift dining tent, our African hosts served us a bowl of hot, thick, creamy peanut soup. Until then, I had had peanuts in only three forms: simply roasted peanuts, boiled peanuts bought at gas stations and roadside stands in Alabama, and peanut butter. That soup in Tanzania was a revelation, my introduction to the peanut's savory possibilities.

Though we tend to treat peanuts like other nuts because of their similar flavor and texture, they're actually a legume, more closely related to the lima bean than the cashew. A New World tropical native probably first domesticated in South America, the peanut was grown by pre-Columbian cultures for generations. Like field peas, peanuts were fed to livestock more often than to humans in the United States in colonial days. The popularization of peanut butter around 1900 changed that forever.

Peanuts are most often incorporated into sweet dishes in the South. Think peanut butter cookies and peanut butter pie. My nods to that sweet tradition are a simple peanut brittle made with high quality chocolate and a peanut-banana tart made with puff pastry. Boiled peanuts, of course, are a savory Southern staple, made popular outside the South by the Lee Brothers' catalog and cookbooks. Here, I include a Chinese variation on boiled peanuts, infused with ginger, star anise, and dried red chiles.

Peanuts were introduced to Asia during the Columbian exchange (the exchange of plants, animals, and culture between the Americas, Africa, and Eurasia after 1492), and since then have figured prominently in a variety of sweet and savory preparations from China to Indonesia. Thailand's classic *som tum* salad is made on the streets by women pounding green papaya combined with fish sauce and lime juice in their mortar and pestles, with peanuts as a standard crunchy topping. In this chapter, I merge that dish with cabbage for an Asian-inspired slaw.

In both West Africa and Southeast Asia, peanuts are incorporated into curries, soups, and stews as a thickener. Peanut sauce—a traditional accompaniment to spring rolls in Vietnam and to satays in Singapore and Indonesia—is one of my favorite savory peanut incarnations. One of the best meals I had during a recent trip to Singapore was from a beachside food pavilion: An assortment of charcoal-grilled lamb, chicken, and beef satays was simply served with a spicy peanut sauce and a freezing cold tiger beer.

⸙ Chinese-Style Boiled Peanuts ⸙

Warm, salty boiled peanuts conjure up for me the smell of the South Alabama summertime air. Growing up, I always thought of them as distinctly Southern. But, if we had actually dug that imaginary hole through the earth straight to China when we were little, we would have found Chinese kids snacking on boiled peanuts, too. This could have been their version.

Rinse the peanuts well by covering them with water in a large container, stirring to dislodge any sand or soil, draining, and repeating several times. Combine all the ingredients in a large, heavy saucepan over medium-high heat, cover, and bring to a boil. Reduce to a simmer and cook, stirring often and adding more water as needed. After 1½ hours, taste a couple of peanuts of different sizes for doneness and for saltiness. If you would like them saltier, add an additional 1 tablespoon (18 g) of salt. Cook an additional 30 minutes to 2 hours depending on the peanuts' size, or until they are as soft as you'd like them to be. Let the peanuts cool in their cooking liquid, then drain, and discard the star anise, chile, and ginger. Keep refrigerated, covered, for up to 3 days.

YIELD: 1½ POUNDS (**680** g)

1 pound (455 g) raw, unshelled green peanuts

3 tablespoons (54 g) kosher salt, or more to taste

5 cups (1.2 L) water

1 whole star anise

1 dried red chile

1 piece fresh ginger, 3-inches (7.5 cm) long, peeled and sliced

2 tablespoons (30 ml) rice wine vinegar

2 tablespoons (26 g) granulated sugar

❧ Som Tum Slaw ❧

This is a Thai-style take on Southern coleslaw, inspired by the classic som tum salad and its balance of spicy, sweet, sour, and salty. In Bangkok and throughout Thailand, women pound som tum in their big wooden mortar and pestles. Peanuts are classic in som tum and lend that salad and this slaw richness and crunch.

In a large, sturdy, preferably wooden bowl, combine the chiles, garlic, shallot, and green beans. Mash these ingredients together with the back of a spoon just until the green beans are bruised and infused with flavor. In a small bowl, whisk together the fish sauce and sugar, add to the green beans, and stir to coat. Add the cabbage and lime juice, and stir for a few minutes to mix all the ingredients together. Add the tomatoes, peanuts, and herbs, and stir to combine. The final salad should be a good balance of sweet, salty, and sour, so add more fish sauce and lime juice as needed, stirring to incorporate all the flavors until you like the balance.

YIELD: 6 TO 8 SERVINGS

2 Thai chiles, seeds and ribs removed for less heat, minced

1 tablespoon (10 g) minced garlic

1 teaspoon (3 g) minced shallot

1 pound (455 g) green beans (any variety)

1 tablespoon (15 ml) fish sauce, plus more to taste

1 teaspoon (15 g) palm sugar or light brown sugar

1 head green or red cabbage, thinly sliced

2 tablespoons (30 ml) lime juice, plus more to taste

8 to 10 cherry tomatoes, quartered

1/2 cup (75 g) roasted and unsalted or lightly salted peanuts

2 tablespoons (2.5 g) thinly sliced fresh basil, cilantro, or mint

✤ Lamb Satay with Peanut Sauce ✤

These kebabs are inspired by one of my favorite food pavilions on a beach in Singapore where the cooking is a mix of Arab, Indian, Chinese, and Malay. Most nights they make kebabs and satays of all kinds, grilled over hardwood charcoal and served with spicy peanut sauce on the side. The spice mix below is especially good with lamb, but also works well with beef, chicken, or pork.

To make the kebabs: Toast the cumin and coriander seeds in a dry skillet over medium heat 2 to 4 minutes until fragrant. Grind them in a spice grinder or mortar and pestle, and combine with the cayenne, salt, turmeric, and sugar in a small bowl. If using cubed lamb, combine the lamb and spices in a food processor and pulse until ground. If using ground lamb, use your hands to mix the spices and lamb together.

Divide the lamb among 6 large, preferably flat, stainless steel skewers, or among 18 to 20 wooden skewers that have been soaked in warm water for at least 1 hour. Pressing and squeezing the lamb so that it adheres to the skewers.

To make the peanut sauce: Place the peanuts, garlic, chile, soy sauce, chili sauce or ketchup, canola oil, sugar, lime juice, and sesame oil in a food processor and purée until smooth. Season to taste with salt and pepper.

Preheat the grill to high. Cook the lamb, turning once or twice, 6 to 8 minutes, or until lamb is just cooked through. Serve with the peanut sauce.

YIELD: **4 TO 6 SERVINGS**

For the kebabs:

2 teaspoons (2 g) whole cumin seeds

2 teaspoons (3.6 g) whole coriander seeds

1 teaspoon (1.8 g) cayenne pepper, or to taste

1½ teaspoons (9 g) kosher salt

2 teaspoons (4.4 g) ground turmeric

2 teaspoons (10 g) palm sugar or light brown sugar

2 pounds (905 g) lamb shoulder, cubed, or ground lamb

For the peanut sauce:

½ cup (75 g) roasted and unsalted or lightly salted peanuts

1 clove garlic, peeled

1 Thai or jalapeño chile

2 tablespoons (30 ml) soy sauce

2 tablespoons (30 ml) sweet chili sauce or ketchup

2 tablespoons (30 ml) canola oil

3 tablespoons (45 g) palm sugar or light brown sugar

2 teaspoons (10 ml) lime juice

¼ teaspoon toasted sesame oil

Kosher salt and freshly ground black pepper

❧ Beef, Potato, and Peanut Curry ❧

Peanuts are often incorporated into Southeast Asian dishes for richness and texture. In this stew, peanuts thicken the broth, give body to the stew, and help carry the bold flavors of the curry paste. You can substitute store-bought red curry paste for the recipe below.

Season the beef generously with kosher salt, and refrigerate for at least one hour and up to 24 hours.

To make the curry paste: Toast the cumin and coriander seeds, peppercorns, and cloves in a dry skillet over medium heat, stirring often, 2 to 4 minutes, or until fragrant. Transfer spices to a bowl. Toast the cinnamon, nutmeg, and cardamom in the same dry skillet, stirring constantly, about 1 minute, until fragrant. Grind the toasted whole spices in a spice grinder or mortar and pestle, then combine with the salt and ground spices, and set aside.

For a less spicy stew, remove and discard the seeds and ribs from the chiles. Trim and discard the top green part and tough bottom part of the lemongrass stalk, leaving a piece about 3-inches (7.5 cm) long. Remove and discard the two outer layers, then finely mince the remaining interior part of the lemongrass.

Combine the chiles, lemongrass, ginger, garlic, shallot, and shrimp paste with the ground spice mixture in a mortar and pestle or food processor, and pound or process until very smooth.

To make the stew: Bring the coconut milk to a boil in a large, heavy stockpot over medium-high heat. Reduce to a simmer, and cook 3 to 5 minutes, or until reduced by half. Stir in the curry paste and cook, stirring often, 3 minutes. Add the chicken stock, star anise, kaffir lime leaves, fish sauce, sugar, and lime juice, and bring to a boil. Add the beef, stir, and reduce to a simmer, then cover, and cook, stirring occasionally, for 30 minutes. Add the onion, potatoes, and peanuts, and cook another 30 to 60 minutes, or until the beef is tender and the potatoes are cooked through. Remove and discard the kaffir lime leaves and star anise. Add more lime juice, to taste, and season to taste with salt and pepper.

YIELD: 4 TO 6 SERVINGS

2 pounds (905 g) beef chuck, cut into 1-inch (2.5 cm) pieces

Kosher salt

For the curry paste:

2 teaspoons (2 g) whole cumin seeds

1 teaspoon (2 g) whole coriander seeds

1 teaspoon (2 g) black peppercorns

2 whole cloves

1/2 teaspoon ground cinnamon

1/2 teaspoon ground nutmeg

1/2 teaspoon ground cardamom

1 teaspoon (6 g) kosher salt

4 Thai chiles

2 stalks fresh lemongrass

4 teaspoons (8 g) minced, peeled fresh ginger

2 teaspoons (6 g) minced garlic

2 tablespoons (6 g) minced shallot

2 teaspoons (10 g) shrimp paste (optional)

For the stew:

4 cups (945 ml) coconut milk

4 cups (945 ml) chicken stock

1 whole star anise

4 kaffir lime leaves

2 tablespoons (30 ml) fish sauce, or 4 tablespoons (60 ml) if omitting shrimp paste

2 tablespoons (30 g) palm sugar or light brown sugar

2 tablespoons (30 ml) lime juice, plus more to taste

1 yellow onion, cut into wedges

1 1/2 pounds (680 g) waxy potatoes (such as red potatoes), peeled and cut into 1-inch (2.5 cm) pieces

1 cup (145 g) coarsely chopped roasted unsalted or lightly salted peanuts

Salt and freshly ground black pepper

❧ Peanut Chicken and Vegetable Stew ❧

I had my first savory peanut stew on a three-week safari in Africa. The dish seemed odd at first—I was mostly accustomed to peanuts either boiled, roasted, or as peanut butter—but it inspired me to start incorporating peanuts into savory dishes at home. This stew is based on one you might find in West Africa, where peanuts are an important source of protein. They lend a rich flavor and silky texture to the stew.

Season the chicken pieces all over with salt and cayenne pepper, and set aside for 20 minutes.

Heat the oil in a large, heavy stockpot over medium-high heat. Add the chicken and cook, turning once or twice, 2 to 4 minutes, or until browned on all sides. Transfer the chicken to a plate.

Add the onion, allspice, ginger, turmeric, and cardamom to the pot along with a light sprinkling of salt and cayenne pepper. Cook, stirring often, for 3 minutes. Add the tomato paste and cook, stirring often, 2 to 4 minutes, or until the tomato paste darkens in color. Add the garlic and cook 30 seconds. Add the tomatoes, or tomato purée, chicken broth, water, butternut squash, and turnip, and bring to a boil, then reduce to a simmer.

In a small bowl, whisk together the peanut butter, sugar, and 1 cup (235 ml) of the simmering cooking liquid; whisk this mixture back into the stew.

Simmer, stirring occasionally, 10 to 15 minutes, or until the butternut squash is just tender. Add the chicken to the pot, bring to a boil, and then turn off the heat. When the chicken is just cooked through, after 6 to 8 minutes, stir in the mint and season to taste with salt and cayenne pepper.

YIELD: **4** TO **6** SERVINGS

4 boneless, skinless chicken breasts halves, cut into bite-size pieces

Kosher salt and cayenne pepper

2 tablespoons (30 ml) canola oil

2 yellow onions, chopped

1 teaspoon (2 g) ground allspice

½ teaspoon ground ginger

2 teaspoons (4.4 g) ground turmeric

1 teaspoon (2 g) ground cardamom

¼ cup (65 g) tomato paste

4 cloves garlic, minced

2 cups (360 g) diced tomatoes or 2 cups (500 g) tomato purée

4 cups (945 ml) chicken broth

4 cups (945 ml) water

2 butternut squash, peeled and cut into bite-size pieces

1 small turnip, peeled and cut into bite-size pieces

1 cup (260 g) smooth unsweetened peanut butter

2 tablespoons (30 g) palm sugar or brown sugar

2 tablespoons (12 g) finely chopped fresh mint

❧ Chocolate and Sea Salt Peanut Brittle ❧

A few small pieces of good-quality chocolate or a handful of nuts are often my go-to easy dessert. This brittle combines the two and only takes a little more work.

Place a metal or glass bowl over a large saucepan filled halfway with water to make a double boiler. Bring the water to boil, and then reduce it to a gentle simmer. Place the chocolate and corn syrup in the bowl, and cook, stirring often, until melted and smooth. Stir in the peanuts and immediately pour this mixture out onto a sheet pan lined with parchment paper or a silicone baking mat. Using a spatula, evenly disperse the peanuts and spread the mixture into an even thickness. Sprinkle with the salt. Refrigerate until hardened, then break or cut into pieces for serving.

YIELD: ½ POUND (225 g) OF BRITTLE

8 ounces (225 g) 70% dark chocolate, roughly chopped

2 teaspoons (44 g) corn syrup

1 cup (145 g) roasted unsalted peanuts

½ teaspoon sea salt

❧ **Peanut and Banana Tart** ❧

This tart is a refined take on the old-school peanut butter and banana sandwich. When the peanut butter cooks a little with the sugar to make the tart filling, it takes on a chocolatey flavor. Puff pastry makes for a delicately crunchy and buttery foundation.

1 sheet puff pastry, thawed overnight in fridge

7 to 9 barely ripe bananas, halved lengthwise

1 tablespoon (15 ml) lemon juice

½ cup (100 g) granulated sugar

3 tablespoons (42 g) unsalted butter

2 tablespoons (32 g) peanut butter

2 tablespoons (30 ml) water

Pinch salt

2 tablespoons (18 g) coarsely chopped roasted unsalted peanuts

Preheat the oven to 375°F (190°C, or gas mark 5).

Remove the puff pastry from the refrigerator and roll it to an even thickness on a lightly floured surface. Trim away a ¾-inch (19 mm) border from the edges of the puff pastry. Lay these strips on top of the puff pastry along the outside edges, press them to adhere, and trim away any excess, yielding a roughly 8 x 12-inch (20 x 30 cm) tart base. Slide the puff pastry onto a piece of parchment paper or silicone baking mat, and transfer to a large rimmed baking sheet. Bake 15 to 20 minutes, or until puffed and golden brown. Remove from the oven and allow to cool slightly. Increase the oven to 425° (220°C, or gas mark 7).

In a large bowl, gently toss the bananas with the lemon juice, then arrange them cut side-up on the puff pastry. Place the pastry nearby as you proceed to the next step, because the next step will happen quickly.

Melt the sugar in a medium-size saucepan over medium heat, stirring often. When the sugar melts, cook without stirring for 1 to 2 minutes, or until it turns amber in color. Working quickly, remove the pan from the heat to cool slightly, then whisk in the butter, peanut butter, water, and pinch of salt until smooth, adding a little bit more water if necessary so the mixture is pourable. Drizzle this mixture evenly over and around the bananas. Sprinkle the peanuts evenly over the bananas. Bake 10 to 15 minutes, or until the bananas are hot.

YIELD: **6** TO **8** SERVINGS

PECANS

A variety of hickory native to North America, pecans have grown in the southeastern United States for eons. With an appearance and flavor similar to the walnut, the pecan is packed with nutrition for its weight and was a staple food of Native Americans long before Europeans settled in the South.

My paternal grandfather grew up on a farm in Barbour County, Alabama, in the southern part of the state where pecan trees thrive. He kept a grove his whole life, and every year the business he started sends fresh pecans to friends and employees as a reminder of those origins. At their house in Birmingham, my grandparents always seemed to have a bowl of unshelled pecans in the living room, with a variety of nutcrackers within reach.

I live now in what used to be a pecan grove on Sullivan's Island, just outside of Charleston. I have four pecan trees in my yard, and my neighbors each have one or two. They're old trees and lose a handful of branches every summer, but they still produce loads of pecans every other year. I always have plenty of pecans on hand—too many really—which means I'm always looking for ways to incorporate them into my cooking, from breakfast to dinner, sweet to savory.

How to describe the flavor of a pecan? Where walnuts tend to have a little astringent bitterness when they're raw, pecans have a buttery, more balanced flavor, and a warm, comforting, woodsy aroma. The meat of the pecan has a softer texture than the walnut, with just a little resistance to the tooth. When toasted, the pecan's flavor becomes more complex and concentrated, and it gets crunchier.

For basic roasted pecans, I preheat the oven to 275°F (140°C, or gas mark 1), arrange the pecans in a single layer on a large sheet pan, and roast them for 30 to 45 minutes, stirring and tasting occasionally, until I find the flavor I'm looking for. Sometimes I toast them in a dry skillet. Room for variation is infinite when roasting pecans, and they're delicious tossed with just about any fat (butter, olive oil, walnut oil), any ground spice (cinnamon, curry powder, cumin), and any sweetener (sugar, honey, molasses). Flavorful condiments like soy sauce and hot sauce add even more flavor.

Pecans are most often incorporated into sweet dishes in the South, such as pecan pie (a version of which I infuse here with chocolate), and in the famous pralines popular in New Orleans. They're good in cookies, too, especially when complemented by warm spices such as cardamom. I like to sprinkle toasted, crumbled pecans over ice cream and fruit desserts to add texture and flavor, and over sweet breakfast dishes such as oatmeal and quinoa. Pecans are a natural match with cheese, too, since they have a similar richness but with a crunchy texture. I love throwing them into salads, sautéing or roasting them with vegetables, and combining them with panko as crust for meat and fish.

❧ Breakfast Quinoa with Bananas, Blueberries, Honey, and Pecans ❧

Quinoa is one of my favorite grains—I love its fine texture and nutty flavor. I like to treat it as oatmeal for breakfast such as in this version with bananas, fresh blueberries, and pecans. It's a great way to use leftover quinoa, too.

Toast the quinoa in a medium-size saucepan over medium heat, stirring often, until dry and lightly toasted, 3 to 5 minutes. Add the salt and water, stir, cover the pot, bring to a boil, and then reduce to a simmer. Cook, covered, about 10 minutes, or until the quinoa is tender and you can see its tail-like tendril.

Meanwhile, toast the pecan pieces in a dry skillet for 2 to 4 minutes, or until the pecans are lightly browned. Transfer the pecans to a plate to cool.

Uncover the quinoa and stir to let most of the water evaporate. Stir in the garam masala, or cinnamon, ½ cup (120 ml) of the milk, the raisins, currants, or cranberries, and the butter. Cook, stirring frequently, about 2 minutes, or until most of the milk has evaporated. Add the remaining 1 cup (235 ml) milk, the honey, blueberries, banana, and one-half of the pecans. Fold the quinoa together for 3 to 5 minutes, or until it reaches the desired consistency. Garnish with the remaining pecans.

YIELD: 2 TO 4 SERVINGS

1 cup (173 g) quinoa, rinsed and drained

Pinch salt

1¼ cups (295 ml) water

⅔ cup (73 g) pecans, broken into pieces

½ teaspoon garam masala or cinnamon

1½ (295 ml) cups milk, divided

½ cup (75 g) raisins, or dried currants or cranberries

2 tablespoons (28 g) unsalted butter

1 teaspoon (7 g) honey

1 cup (145 g) fresh blueberries

1 banana, sliced

❧ Pecan Habañero Pimento Cheese ❧

Pimento cheese, of course, is a southern classic and one that I've been eating since I can remember. This nontraditional version is made with Monterey Jack rather than cheddar with fruity and hot habañeros and pecans for a nutty texture and flavor. Add more or less mayonnaise and lemon juice to make the pimento cheese as spreadable as you like.

Combine the habañero, red peppers or pimento, cheese, pecans, red peppers, mayonnaise, lemon juice, and chives in a large bowl, and stir to combine. Season to taste with salt and pepper. Refrigerate for up to 1 week, and let come to room temperature before serving.

YIELD: About 1½ cups (345 g)

½ habañero chile, seeds and ribs removed for less heat, minced, or use cayenne pepper or red pepper flakes to taste

½ pound (225 g) Monterey Jack cheese, grated

½ cup (50 g) pecans, coarsely chopped

¼ cup (45 g) diced roasted red peppers or jarred pimientos, drained

½ cup (115 g) mayonnaise

3 tablespoon (45 ml) freshly squeezed lemon juice

2 teaspoons (2 g) minced fresh chives

Salt and pepper

ᘒ **Kale, Apple, and Pecan Salad with Black Benne Dressing** ᘒ

In this bright raw salad, apples add a little sweetness to the slightly bitter kale, and the pecans add buttery flavor. The dressing is inspired by a sweet poppy seed dressing but with benne seeds instead—an oft forgotten old Southern ingredient. Dijon mustard balances everything out.

To make the dressing: Combine the cider vinegar and shallot in a medium-size bowl, along with a light sprinkling of salt. Set aside for 10 minutes, and then add the honey, mustard, benne seeds, and olive oil, and whisk to combine. Season to taste with salt and pepper.

To make the salad: Break the pecans into pieces and toast them in a dry skillet over medium heat for 2 to 4 minutes, or until lightly browned. In a large bowl, toss the kale and apples with the dressing, and garnish with more pecans and benne seeds. Season to taste with salt and pepper.

YIELD: 4 TO 6 SERVINGS

For the dressing:

3 tablespoons (45 ml) apple cider vinegar

1 medium shallot, minced (about 1 tablespoon, or 15 g)

Kosher salt and freshly ground black pepper

2 tablespoons (40 g) honey

3 teaspoons (12 g) Dijon mustard

3 teaspoons (8 g) black benne seeds (sesame seeds), plus more for garnish

2 tablespoons (30 ml) olive oil

For the salad:

½ cup pecans (50 g), plus more for garnish

24 ounces (745 g) Lacinato kale (also called black kale and dinosaur kale), stemmed and thinly sliced

1 Granny Smith apple, cut into matchsticks

1 Braeburn or Fuji apple, cut into matchsticks

Kosher salt and freshly ground black pepper

❧ Roasted Brussels Sprouts with Country Ham, Pecans, and Avocado ❧

This combination of colorful ingredients is inspired by one of Jean-Georges Vongerichten's recipes that I first read about in *Food & Wine* magazine. Brussels sprouts and pecans have always gone well together, but the addition of creamy, warmed avocado works surprisingly well.

Preheat the oven to 350°F (180°C, or gas mark 4). Toast the pecans on a baking sheet about 5 minutes, or until lightly browned and fragrant. Transfer to a plate to cool. Increase the oven temperature to 400°F (200°C, or gas mark 6).

In a large bowl, toss the Brussels sprouts and country ham with the olive oil, season with salt and red pepper flakes (keep in mind that the country ham is already salty), and spread evenly on a large baking sheet. Roast 15 to 20 minutes, or until the Brussels sprouts are brown in spots and cooked through.

Transfer the Brussels sprouts and country ham to a bowl, toss with the avocado and thyme, and season to taste with salt and pepper. Top with the toasted pecans, and drizzle with the balsamic vinegar.

YIELD: 4 TO 6 SERVINGS

½ cup pecans (50 g), roughly halved

2 pounds (905 g) Brussels sprouts, stem ends trimmed away and discarded, outer leaves discarded, halved

6 ounces (170 g) country ham, cut into 1-inch (2.5 cm) squares

2 tablespoons (30 ml) olive oil

¼ teaspoon kosher salt, or to taste

¼ teaspoon red pepper flakes, or to taste

1½ medium avocado, diced

1 teaspoon (.8 g) chopped fresh thyme

Balsamic vinegar, for drizzling (optional)

❧ **Pecan and Herb-Crusted Pork Chops** ❧

Pecans make a great crust for chicken and pork. Even though they're baked, these chops come away with a fried-like texture and flavor thanks to the pecans and a little butter. I like to serve these with a simple, bright salad of fennel and radicchio dressed with a splash of lemon juice and olive oil.

4 boneless pork loin chops, 2-inches (5 cm) thick each

Kosher salt and freshly ground black pepper

1 cup (100 g) pecans

4 tablespoons (56 g) unsalted butter

1 medium-size shallot, minced

1 cup panko (50 g) bread crumbs

¼ teaspoon minced fresh thyme

¼ teaspoon minced fresh rosemary

¼ teaspoon cayenne pepper

3 eggs

2 teaspoons (8 g) Dijon mustard

1 cup (125 g) all-purpose flour

Season the pork chops on both sides with salt and pepper, and allow them to come to room temperature. Preheat the oven to 350°F (180°C, or gas mark 4).

Pulse the pecans several times in a food processor until about the same consistency as the panko bread crumbs. Alternatively, place them in a plastic bag and pound them with a meat tenderizer until ground.

Melt the butter in a large skillet over medium heat. Cook, swirling the pan, 2 to 4 minutes, or until the butter turns golden brown. (Watch carefully because this can happen quickly.) Add the shallot and a light sprinkling of salt, and cook, stirring occasionally, 2 to 4 minutes, or until the shallots are soft. Reduce the heat to low, add the panko and pecans and cook, stirring occasionally, 8 to 10 minutes, or until golden brown. Transfer this mixture to a bowl, and stir in the thyme, rosemary, and cayenne pepper.

Whisk together the eggs and mustard in a shallow dish. Place the flour in another shallow dish. One at a time, first dip the pork chops in the flour and shake off the excess; then into the egg and mustard mixture and allow the excess drain away; and then into the pecan and panko mixture, pressing to coat the chops evenly.

Place the pork chops on a sheet pan (preferably lined with a wire rack), and bake 20 to 30 minutes, or until just cooked through. Let rest 10 minutes before serving.

YIELD: **4** SERVINGS

❧ Chocolate Pecan Pie ❧

The addition of good-quality chocolate to an already decadent pecan pie is, well, even more decadent. Adding vodka to the pie dough is a trick I learned from the folks at America's Test Kitchen; it makes the crust extra flaky and light.

To make the dough: Combine the flour, sugar, and salt in a food processor or in a bowl, and pulse once or twice or stir to combine. Add the butter and shortening, and process about 10 seconds, or until the butter pieces are the size of small peas. Transfer the mixture to a mixing bowl, and stir in the water and vodka until just combined and a little sticky, adding a little more or less water as needed. Roll the dough into a ball, cover with plastic wrap, and refrigerate for at least 30 minutes and up to 2 days.

Let the dough sit at room temperature for 15 minutes, then roll out on a floured work surface into a circle roughly 12 inches (30 cm) round and ⅛-inch (3 mm) thick. Place the dough over a 9-inch (23 cm) pie pan, and press the dough into the pan without stretching it. Trim away the dough from around the edge of the pan leaving ½ inch overhanging; crimp the edges by folding the dough onto itself at increments. Refrigerate about 30 minutes, or until firm.

Preheat the oven to 375°F (190°C, or gas mark 5), and place the rack in the middle position. Remove the crust from the refrigerator, line the crust with foil, fill with dried beans or coins, and bake 15 minutes. Remove the foil and beans, and bake 5 to10 more minutes, or until the crust is light brown. Set aside to cool slightly.

To make the filling: Place the chocolate and butter in a bowl set over a saucepan filled with simmering water, and stir until melted (or melt the chocolate and butter together in a microwave). Transfer the chocolate to a mixing bowl, add the sugar, eggs, corn syrup, vanilla extract, and salt, and stir until combined and smooth.

To make the pie: Pour the filling into the crust. Arrange the pecans on top of the filling, pressing so they adhere to the filling. Bake 30 to 45 minutes, or until the pie is set in the center. Let cool completely before serving.

YIELD: ONE **9-INCH (23 cm)** PIE

For the dough:

2 cups (250 g) all-purpose flour, plus more for dusting

2 teaspoons (8 g) granulated sugar

½ teaspoon kosher salt

¾ cup (167 g) chilled unsalted butter, cut into ¼-inch (6 mm) pieces

½ cup (100 g) chilled vegetable shortening, cut into large pieces

2 tablespoons (30 ml) ice water

2 tablespoons (30 ml) cold vodka

For the filling:

6 ounces (170 g) 70% cacao chocolate, broken into several large pieces

4 tablespoons (55 g) unsalted butter

¾ cup (150 g) raw sugar

3 eggs, beaten

½ cup (170 g) light corn syrup

1 teaspoon (5 ml) vanilla extract

Pinch kosher salt

1 to 2 cups pecans

❧ Oatmeal Pecan Cardamom Cookies ❧

I love a classic oatmeal cookie, especially when pecans are involved. The addition of cardamom and lemon zest gives these a spicy brightness that makes them seem not as sweet as most cookies but equally as flavorful. They're delicious with a cup of green tea or a bourbon on the rocks.

½ cup (55 g) coarsely chopped pecans

1 cup (225 g) unsalted butter, just below room temperature

1 cup (225 g) packed light brown sugar

1 cup (200 g) granulated sugar

2 eggs

1½ cups (63 g) all-purpose flour

½ teaspoon fine salt

½ teaspoon baking powder

¼ teaspoon freshly grated nutmeg

¼ teaspoon ground cardamom

½ teaspoon finely grated lemon zest

2 eggs, beaten

3 cups (240 g) rolled oats

Preheat the oven to 350°F (180°C, or gas mark 4), and place the rack in the middle position. Place the pecans on a baking sheet and bake about 5 minutes, or until toasted.

Cream the butter using a stand mixer or by hand until fluffy. Add the light brown sugar and granulated sugar, and mix until the sugar is thoroughly dissolved. Add in the eggs one at a time, and mix until just incorporated.

Transfer the mixture to a mixing bowl, and stir in the flour, salt, baking powder, nutmeg, cardamom, lemon zest, beaten eggs, and rolled oats. Line a baking sheet with parchment paper or a silicone baking mat. Form the dough into 1- to 2-inch (2.5 to 5 cm) balls (an ice cream scoop works well for this), and arrange them on the baking sheet with plenty of room between them.

Bake, rotating the pan once, 20 to 25 minutes, or until the cookies are golden brown and still chewy.

YIELD: 15 TO 20 COOKIES

❧ Buttermilk Pecan Ice Cream ❧

Butter pecan ice cream is, of course, a classic. Buttermilk makes this version Southern-inspired and balances out the richness with a little bit of tang. Any ice cream maker works for this—just follow the manufacturer's instructions. You'll probably need to firm up the finished ice cream in the freezer, and then let it soften some when fresh out of the freezer before serving.

1 cup (200 g) granulated sugar, divided

2 cups (475 ml) heavy cream

1 vanilla bean, split in half

10 large egg yolks

2 cups (475 ml) whole buttermilk

Pinch salt

Optional garnish:

Peanuts, coarsley chopped

Place ¾ cup (150 g) of the sugar and the heavy cream in a large, heavy saucepan, and scrape the vanilla bean seeds into this mixture. Add the scraped vanilla bean pod to this mixture, and bring to a simmer over medium-high heat.

Whisk together the egg yolks and the remaining ¼ cup (50 g) sugar until the sugar is dissolved. When the heavy cream mixture simmers, remove it from the heat, and discard the vanilla bean pod. Very slowly pour ½ cup (120 ml) or so of this mixture into the egg yolk mixture in a thin stream, whisking constantly to prevent the egg yolks from curdling.

Whisk this mixture back into the saucepan with the heavy cream mixture, whisking constantly. Simmer gently, stirring constantly, until mixture is thick enough to coat the back of a spoon. Whisk in the buttermilk and pinch of salt, and stir to combine.

Freeze in an ice cream maker according to the manufacturer's directions.

YIELD: 1 QUART (1.1 kg)

FIGS

Tenacious, drought-tolerant fig trees lend a touch of the bucolic wherever they manage to grow: hanging over an entryway, clinging to a narrow strip of soil in a back alley, or thriving in an open field. The fig's lobed green leaf, grey bark, and unmistakable teardrop-shaped fruit are familiar to most, and the fig is probably so widely cultivated because the tree itself is much more resilient than its quick-ripening soft-fleshed fruit.

Summers when I was young, we'd drive from Birmingham to the beach and find fresh fig preserves at roadside farm stands. The high sugar content and short shelf life of fresh figs make them ideal for preserving, whether to slather on a buttery biscuit or to spread on a whole-grain cracker with almond butter for breakfast. I also like to turn figs into sweet and salty chutneys, delicious with roasted and grilled meats or spread like jam on a good piece of bread.

Figs have an affinity for the heat of the South, in part because their protective skin and broad resilient leaves give them the ability to withstand the varying dry, hot, and wet conditions. The unusually coarse texture of a fig's skin is explained by the fact that the fig isn't a fruit at all but an elongated stem, which attracts pollinators to its multitude of tiny seed-like interior flowers. That stem attracts birds, too, as I've found every time I've tried to grow a fig tree at my home on Sullivan's Island, where planting figs just doesn't seem to be worth the effort.

Though they grow well in the South, figs are also happy in arid climates, where the dry summers and cool nights concentrate their flavor. In Italy, fresh figs are wrapped in prosciutto, grilled, added to pizzas and crostinis, and incorporated into simple cakes that are less sweet than American versions. In the South of France, they're blended into black olive tapenades, and simply roasted and adorned with honey. And in North Africa and their native Middle East where sweet and sour preparations are common, dried figs are added to spiced stews and tagines, rice dishes, and are reconstituted for simple dried fruit salads.

Today the largest concentrations of fig trees are in the arid climates of Turkey, Italy, Spain, Greece, and California. Black Mission figs, fresh or dried, have dark blue to purple skin and a sweet, dark jammy flavor. Calimyrna figs have lighter green to yellow skins and a nutty, honey-like flavor when dried. I especially love dried Calimyrnas on their own, as a quick dessert, or stuffed with goat cheese for a simple appetizer. Brown Turkeys are a larger variety, and Kadotas are the most common green fig.

❦ Quick Fig Jam ❦

This is an easy and delicious way to preserve an abundance of fresh figs. You can increase or decrease the heat and cooking time so the jam is as thin or as thick as you like, and even purée it in a food processor. It's a good alternative to the more involved canning process.

Combine all the ingredients in a medium-size saucepan. Bring to a simmer over medium heat, adding a little water if the figs don't release enough liquid themselves. Cook, stirring frequently and adjusting the heat to prevent scorching, 8 to 10 minutes, or until the mixture is a thick jam consistency. Let cool completely, and store in an airtight container for up to a week.

YIELD: 1 TO 2 CUPS (320 TO 640 g)

About 20 fresh figs, stems removed

¼ cup (50 g) granulated sugar

¼ cup (85 g) honey

2 tablespoons (28 ml) fresh lemon juice

2 teaspoons (1.6 g) minced fresh thyme

Herb Grilled Bison Rib Eyes with Onion, Tomato, and Fig Chutney

I love the bold, natural flavor of bison, often raised on grasses—their native diet. The combined flavors of onion, tomato, and figs are delicious with the bison. A few crumbled pieces of blue cheese would add even more flavor.

To make the chutney: Preheat the oven to 250°F (120°C, or gas mark ½). Put the tomatoes and thyme sprigs on a sheet pan, drizzle with 2 teaspoons (10 ml) of olive oil, season lightly with salt and pepper, and roast about 1½ hours, or until the tomatoes are almost completely dried and their flavors concentrated.

Put the figs in a small saucepan, cover with the water, and simmer about 30 minutes, or until tender. Drain, reserving the cooking liquid. Place the cooking liquid in a small saucepan over medium heat, and simmer until reduced to about ¼ cup (60 ml). Cut off and discard the figs' stems, and cut them into quarters lengthwise.

Place the onions, the remaining 2 tablespoons (30 ml) of olive oil, and the 1 teaspoon (6 g) kosher salt in a large skillet and cook over medium heat, tightly covered, stirring occasionally, about 1 hour, or until the onions are tender, light brown, and sweet. You may need to add a little water to the skillet to keep the onions from browning too much. Stir the tomatoes and figs into the onions, and thin with a little bit of the fig cooking liquid if necessary. Season with salt and pepper to taste.

To cook the rib eyes: Season the rib eyes generously all over with salt and pepper, and set aside for 30 minutes. In a small bowl, mix together the chopped fresh herbs.

Heat the grill to high. Sprinkle the fresh herbs all over both sides of the rib eyes, and press so the herbs stick. Brush the rib eyes with olive oil, and grill over high heat, turning once, until meat thermometer measures 125°F (52°C) for rare or 135°F (57°C) for medium-rare. Let the rib eyes rest, loosely tented with foil, for 10 minutes. Serve with the chutney.

YIELD: **4** TO **6** SERVINGS

For the chutney:

12 cherry tomatoes

2 sprigs fresh thyme

2 tablespoons plus 2 teaspoons (40 ml) olive oil, divided

1 teaspoon (6 g) kosher salt, plus more to taste

Freshly ground black pepper

2 cups (300 g) dried Black Mission figs

2 cups (475 ml) water

1 medium-size yellow onion, sliced

For the bison rib eyes:

4 thick-cut bison rib eyes

3 tablespoons (7 g) any combination of chopped fresh rosemary, thyme, marjoram, or oregano

Kosher salt and freshly ground black pepper

A chutney is a condiment of Indian origin made with a vast array of fresh, pickled, and preserved fruits, vegetables, spices, and chiles, with citrus, vinegar, or yogurt. Adopted and spread westward by the British during Indian colonization, chutneys enliven all kinds of dishes with their assertive sweet, sour, and spicy flavors.

❧ Fig and Black Olive Tapenade ❧

I first had black olive tapenade at a Parisian bistro called Bistro d'Henri, a small, simple Left Bank place where the tables almost touch and the menu is a chalkboard. The tapenade was mounded in the center of the plate surrounded by thinly sliced fresh mozzarella, drizzled with olive oil, and scattered with fresh basil. The contrast between the intensely flavorful tapenade, subtler milky mozzarella, and fruity olive oil is still one of the best food matches I've had. Figs are a Provençal-inspired addition that adds another layer of flavor and a subtle sweetness.

3/4 cup (113 g) dried figs, preferably Black Mission

1 tablespoon (8.6 g) capers, rinsed and drained

2 cups (270 g) black Greek or Niçoise olives, pitted

2 tablespoons (30 ml) fresh lemon juice, plus more to taste

1 small clove garlic

1 anchovy fillet

1/4 teaspoon fresh thyme leaves

1/4 cup (60 ml) olive oil, plus more to taste

Kosher salt and freshly ground white pepper

Optional accompaniments:

Toasted baguette slices

Crackers

Sliced, fresh mozzarella, with torn basil leaves

Put the figs in a saucepan and cover with water; bring the water to a boil, then reduce the heat and simmer about 20 minutes, or until the figs are soft. Drain the figs, cut off and discard the stem, and cut the figs in half. While the figs are simmering, rinse the capers and soak them in water for 20 minutes. Drain.

Transfer the figs to a food processor and add the capers, olives, lemon juice, garlic, anchovy, and thyme. Process until puréed, but still slightly chunky. Transfer the tapenade to a bowl, stir in the olive oil, season to taste with salt and pepper, and add more lemon juice and olive oil, to taste. Set aside for at least 2 hours before serving for the best flavor, and serve at room temperature, with toasted baguette slices or crackers.

YIELD: ABOUT 2 CUPS (800 g)

◉ Tapenade is a Provençal dish likely brought to France with the Greeks. It traditionally consists of puréed black olives, capers, olive oil, anchovies, and sometimes tuna, but there are many variations. Intensely flavorful, tapenade is good as a spread or in cooking, especially to flavor chicken, fish, and vegetables.

❧ Pizza with Figs, Country Ham, and Mustard Greens ❧

This Southern-inspired pizza has a classic dough that when cooked on a pizza stone or steel cooks up amazingly crisp and chewy. The sugar-cured country ham is reminiscent of prosciutto, and the bitterness of the mustards complements the salty ham and sweet figs.

To make the dough: Combine the flour, sugar, and yeast in a food processor, and pulse 3 or 4 times until combined. With the machine running, slowly add the ice water, and process for 10 seconds, or just until all the flour is incorporated. Leave the dough in the food processor for 10 minutes. Add the oil and salt to the dough, and process until a sticky ball of dough forms that comes away from the sides of the food processor.

Transfer the dough to a lightly oiled work surface, and knead for about 30 seconds to ensure that the salt and oil are incorporated. Place the dough into a large, lightly oiled bowl, cover with plastic wrap, and refrigerate for at least 12 hours and up to 2 days. This will allow the dough's flavor to develop.

To make the sauce: Heat the olive oil in a medium-size skillet over medium heat. Add the garlic and thyme, and cook 30 seconds, or until the garlic is fragrant. Add the tomatoes, salt, sugar, and pepper flakes and cook, stirring occasionally, about 5 minutes, or until just thickened. Set aside or refrigerate until ready to use.

To assemble the pizza: Cook the mustard green leaves in salted boiling water about 2 minutes, or until bright green

and tender. Drain the greens, then spread them out on a kitchen towel, and press to remove any excess water.

Place a pizza stone or steel on the middle rack of the oven, and preheat to 500°F (250°C, or gas mark 10) at least 45 minutes for a crispy crust. Place the dough on a well-floured work surface, and press it into a round disk. Gently stretch or roll the dough out to a 12-inch (30 cm) round. Transfer the dough onto a pizza peel or an inverted sheet pan that has been coated with semolina or cornmeal. Put about ½ cup (123 g) of the sauce onto the dough, spreading to coat the dough, leaving a sauce-free edge around the dough.

Distribute the mustard greens and basil leaves over the sauce, and then place the cheese over the greens and basil. This will help protect the greens and basil during cooking. Add the figs and country ham. Bake the pizza until the cheese is melted and the dough is crispy and as charred as you like it, 6 to 8 minutes if you're using a pizza steel, and 8 to 10 minutes if you're using a pizza stone.

YIELD: ONE 13-INCH (33 CM) PIZZA

For the dough:

1½ cups (205 g) bread flour, plus more for dusting the work surface

½ teaspoon granulated sugar

¼ teaspoon instant or rapid-rise yeast

⅔ cup (155 ml) ice water, or less as needed

1½ teaspoons (7.5 ml) olive oil, plus more for the work surface

½ teaspoon kosher salt

For the sauce:

2 teaspoons (10 ml) olive oil

1 clove garlic, minced

¼ teaspoon minced fresh thyme

1 can (14 ounces, or 400 g) whole peeled tomatoes, drained and puréed, or use ¾ cup (175 ml) tomato purée

½ teaspoon kosher salt

½ teaspoon granulated sugar

¼ teaspoon red pepper flakes

For the topping:

½ pound (225 g) mustard greens, separated into leaves

3 fresh basil leaves, torn into pieces

3 ounces (85 g) fresh mozzarella cheese (about 4 slices), torn into pieces

2 dried Calimyrna figs, thinly sliced

2 ounces (55 g) cured country ham or prosciutto, thinly sliced

❧ **Persian Fruit Salad** ❧

I first learned about this Persian salad called *khoshaf* from Alan Davidson and Charlotte Knox's book, *Fruit*. Rose water, a commonly used Middle Eastern flavoring, adds an exotic floral background flavor when used sparingly. I like this salad with all different kinds of dried fruit: figs, apples, peaches, cherries, apricots—really any dried fruit and any nut work well.

Put the dried fruit and rose water in a bowl, adding enough water to cover. Cover the bowl and soak the fruit at room temperature 12 to 24 hours, turning the fruit occasionally, or until it is rehydrated and very tender. Serve the fruit with a little bit of the soaking liquid, drizzled with the yogurt and honey, and sprinkled with pistachios.

YIELD: **4** TO **6** SERVINGS

12 ounces (340 g) mixed dried fruit (figs, apples, peaches, cherries, and apricots)

2 tablespoons (30 ml) rose water

Greek yogurt, thinned with a little water

Honey or pomegranate molasses

Crumbled pistachios

❧ Roasted Figs with Grand Marnier, Lemon, and Mint ❧

This is my kind of dessert, a simple one that relies more on the freshness of a star ingredient than butter and flour. It's versatile, so you can experiment with different liqueurs, citrus zests, herbs, and even types of sugar. These figs are good eaten on their own, with a little yogurt or crème fraîche, over ice cream, on cereal, or just about any way you can think of.

1 tablespoon (15 ml) Grand Marnier

1 tablespoon (20 g) honey

1 pound (455 g) ripe but firm fresh figs

8 to 10 fresh mint leaves

2 tablespoons (12 g) freshly grated lemon zest

Preheat the oven to 425°F (220°C, or gas mark 7). In a small bowl, whisk together the Grand Marnier and honey. Trim off and discard the stem end of the figs, and then cut the figs in half lengthwise. In a large bowl, toss together the Grand Marnier and honey mixture, figs, mint leaves, and lemon zest. Arrange the figs cut side down on a large sheet pan. Roast 20 to 30 minutes, or until tender. Cool before serving.

YIELD: **6 TO 8** SERVINGS

❃ Olive Oil, Orange, and Fig Cake ❃

I finished up my stint in Rome after college with a three-week tour of the lower part of Italy's "boot." I drove from Rome over to Abruzzo, then south through Puglia, Basilicata, Calabria, and back up through Campania. It's a stunning, sparse landscape with obvious ancient Greek and North African influences. This simple dessert is typical of one you'd find in that part of Italy, enjoyed in the afternoon with a nip of white wine.

½ cup (120 ml) extra-virgin olive oil, plus more for oiling the pan

Zest from 4 oranges

Juice from 1 orange

4 eggs

1 teaspoon (6 g) kosher salt

1 cup (200 g) granulated sugar

2 cups (275 g) coarsely ground cornmeal or polenta

2 teaspoons (9.2 g) baking powder

6 fresh Calimyrna figs, stemmed and quartered lengthwise

Preheat the oven to 350°F (180°C, or gas mark 4). Oil a 9-inch (23 cm) round cake pan with olive oil.

Combine the orange zest, orange juice, and olive oil in a small bowl.

Using a stand mixer or an electric hand-held mixer, mix the eggs and salt together for 1 to 2 minutes, or until frothy. With the mixer running, slowly add the sugar, and continue mixing for 1 to 2 minutes, or until the mixture is pale in color.

In a large bowl, whisk together the cornmeal and baking powder. Fold the egg mixture into this cornmeal mixture, stirring until just combined. Fold in the orange and olive oil mixture, stirring until just combined.

Pour this batter into the oiled cake pan. Drop the figs into the batter, pressing some deeper into the batter than others so they're evenly dispersed throughout the cake.

Bake 45 to 60 minutes, or until a paring knife inserted into the center of the cake comes out clean. Let the cake cool in the pan for 10 minutes, then remove the cake from the pan.

YIELD: ONE 9-INCH (23 cm) CAKE

PEACHES

It seems a shame to subject peak-of-summer peaches to the heat of the stove. Their soft, fuzzy exterior and abundant juice are about as good as it gets, whether eaten leaning over the sink or sliced and slipped into a shallow bowl of fresh cold cream. When I do cook peaches, I keep it simple, brushing them with olive oil, grilling or roasting them, and drizzling them with honey or yogurt. Most of the recipes here respect the inherent flavor of the peach by keeping it raw and pairing with just a few complementary ingredients.

The peach was first cultivated in China 10,000 years ago, and from there it made its way into Persia—from which it derived its biological name, *Prunus persica*—westward into Europe, then on to the New World with Spanish explorers. Today, the United States ranks third in peach production after China and Italy, and most of our peaches come from California, South Carolina, and Georgia. The nectarine is botanically the same fruit as the peach, but has smooth skin.

One of the best-tasting peaches I ever ate was on a 100°F (38°C) summer day in California when I was working in the vineyard at a Napa Valley winery. It was perfectly ripe and freshly picked from a tree, its flavor complex from the San Francisco Bay's cooling fog and concentrated from months without rain in the ripening California sun.

They get that good in the South, too, especially when the rainfall is just right.

I grew up eating the peaches of Chilton County, Alabama, and like many southern fruits and vegetables, peaches take me back to summer vacation. On our drive to Florida, we'd stop at place called Peach Park and buy baskets of peaches, okra, field peas, and squash. Our Fourth of July celebrations at the beach weren't complete without a simple peach cobbler and homemade vanilla ice cream. In this chapter, I reinvent that cobbler in a simpler crumble form and add coconut for a hint of tropical flavor.

Peaches pair beautifully with off-the-beaten-path flavors. They smooth out chile-spiked salsas and lend a kind of island flavor to grilled and roasted meats. In a nourishing peach smoothie, fresh ginger gives frozen peaches a nice bite. They're minimally punctuated with an Italian-inspired southern pesto made with mint and pecans, ingredients that are more abundant in the South than Italian basil and pine nuts. I also like balancing out bitter salad lettuces with sweet peaches, along with dots of creamy goat cheese. Simplicity reigns for dessert, too, and in this chapter, I pair peaches with a drizzled sweet reduction of sparkling Moscato wine.

I like to buy peaches as often as possible when they're in season so they're always ripe and not too soft, free of dents and dark spots. It's important to handle them carefully, too, as they easily bruise in a grocery bag. When less-than-ripe peaches are the only ones I can find, I speed up that ripening by placing them stem-side down between two linen napkins until they're just how I want them.

✜ **Peach Ginger Smoothie** ✜

I make smoothies with all kinds of frozen organic fruit It's a convenient and tasty way to get a quick nutritional punch. This one packs about 17 grams of protein per large smoothie, the antioxidant benefits of ginger and cayenne pepper, and the beneficial omega-3 fatty acids of the flaxseeds (which you can't even tell are there).

Combine all the ingredients in a blender and purée until smooth, adding more honey to taste.

YIELD: 18-ounces (532 ml)

½ pound (225 g) frozen peaches

1 unpeeled fresh peach, pitted and cut into pieces

2 teaspoons (5 g) ground flaxseeds

1 cup (230 g) nonfat Greek yogurt

⅛ teaspoon kosher salt

2 round slices unpeeled fresh ginger, or ½ teaspoon ground ginger

2 teaspoons (14 g) honey, plus more to taste

1½ cups (355 ml) skim milk

Pinch cayenne pepper

❧ Buckwheat Pancakes with Peaches, Honey, and Crème Fraîche ❧

I love the heartiness of real buckwheat pancakes, and honey-sweetened peaches go beautifully with them. Low-fat yogurt makes these especially fluffy, and a dollop of crème fraîche at the end adds a silky richness.

Whisk together the buckwheat flour, baking soda, and salt in a large bowl. In a separate bowl, whisk together the eggs, milk, and yogurt. Pour the wet ingredients into the dry ingredients, and mix until combined. Set aside for 20 minutes so the flour can absorb the liquid.

Heat just enough equal parts of the oil and butter in a large nonstick skillet or on a griddle to coat the cooking surface. When hot, ladle 1¼ cupfuls (295 ml) of batter into the skillet for each pancake; cook, turning once when bubbles form on the pancake, 2 to 4 minutes on the first side and 1 to 2 minutes on the second side. Keep warm in an oven on low heat.

Combine the peaches, honey, and a splash of water in a small nonstick skillet. Cook over medium heat, stirring occasionally, 8 to 10 minutes, or until the peaches are soft and the juice and honey reduce to syrup consistency.

Serve the pancakes topped with the peaches and their syrup, a dollop of crème fraîche, and more honey.

YIELD: **4 TO 6** SERVINGS

2 cups (240 g) buckwheat flour

2 teaspoons (5.2 g) baking soda

1 teaspoon (6 g) kosher salt

2 eggs

1½ cups (355 ml) whole milk

2 cups (460 g) low-fat plain yogurt

Vegetable oil

Unsalted butter

4 medium-ripe peaches, peeled, pitted, and sliced, or 16 to 24 frozen peach slices

2 tablespoons (40 g) honey (buckwheat honey if you can find it), plus more to taste

4 to 6 tablespoons (60 to 90 g) crème fraîche

❧ Peaches with Pecan Mint Pesto ❧

In this simple, height-of-the-summer side dish, the season's best peaches are gently tossed with a Southern-influenced pesto made with pecans and mint. The savory, slightly crunchy pesto delightfully contrasts the sweet peaches.

Cut the peaches in half lengthwise working around the pits, twist to separate the halves, then pull or cut out the pits. Cut each half into quarters lengthwise. In a large bowl, toss the peach quarters with 1 tablespoon (15 ml) of the lemon juice.

Combine the mint, pecans, salt, and pepper in a food processor, and pulse until ground but still a little coarse. Transfer the mixture to a bowl, and stir in the olive oil and remaining 1 tablespoon (15 ml) lemon juice. Add more salt, pepper, and olive oil if you like. The pesto should be just loose enough to coat the peaches.

Toss the peach quarters with a little of the pesto at a time, until coated to your liking.

YIELD: **4** TO **6** SERVINGS

4 to 6 medium-ripe peaches

2 tablespoons (30 ml) fresh lemon juice, divided

1 cup (96 g) loosely packed fresh mint leaves

$\frac{1}{2}$ cup (50 g) pecans

$\frac{1}{4}$ teaspoon kosher salt

$\frac{1}{4}$ teaspoon freshly ground black pepper

$\frac{1}{4}$ cup (60 ml) olive oil

❧ Dandelion, Peach, and Goat Cheese Salad ❧

Dandelion greens are a nice change from spinach and arugula. I love their bitter flavor, especially when matched with something sweet. Goat cheese works great in this salad, and I especially love rich and creamy Capricho de Cabra from Spain. This vinaigrette is my go-to for salads.

Preheat the oven to 350°F (180°C, or gas mark 4). Toast the pumpkin seeds on a sheet pan 5 to 7 minutes until fragrant.

Combine the shallot, lemon juice, and salt in a medium-size bowl, whisk to combine, and set aside for 10 minutes. Whisk in the mustard and olive oil until well combined.

Trim away and discard the very bottom part of the dandelion greens' stems. Tear the leaves into pieces and place them in a large salad bowl. Break the goat cheese into small chunks and add it to the dandelion greens.

Cut the peaches in half lengthwise working around the pits, twist to separate the halves, then pull or cut out the pits. Cut each half into quarters lengthwise. Add the peach slices to the bowl with the dandelion greens and goat cheese. Pour the dressing over the salad and toss to combine. Season to taste with freshly ground black pepper. Sprinkle the pumpkin seeds over the salad.

YIELD: **4** TO **6** SERVINGS

4 tablespoons (16 g) pumpkin seeds (pepitas)

½ medium-size shallot, minced (about 2 tablespoons, or 30 g)

4 tablespoons (60 ml) fresh lemon juice

½ teaspoon kosher salt

1 teaspoon (4 g) Dijon mustard

4 tablespoons (60 ml) extra-virgin olive oil

6 ounces (170 g) dandelion greens

4 ounces (115 g) soft goat cheese, preferably Capricho de Cabra

4 small medium-ripe peaches

Freshly ground black pepper

❧ Grilled Pork Tenderloin with Peach Salsa ❧

I love chunky, fresh salsas that act as both a sauce and a side dish alongside grilled meats, especially in summer when you don't want to heat up the kitchen. The vanilla and honey flavors in peaches are especially good with pork.

To make the pork tenderloin: Season the pork generously all over with salt and pepper. In a small bowl, mix together the cumin, coriander, and mustard. Sprinkle this mixture all over the pork, pressing so it sticks to the pork. Set aside for at least 30 minutes or refrigerate for up to 24 hours. Let come to room temperature before grilling.

Heat grill to high. Brush the pork with olive oil, and grill over high heat about 4 minutes per side, or until seared. Transfer the pork to indirect heat, and cook another 10 to 15 minutes, depending on the thickness of the tenderloin, or until meat thermometer reads 145°F (63°C) for medium. Let the pork rest, loosely tented with foil, for 10 minutes before slicing.

To make the salsa: In a small bowl, mix together peaches, tomatoes, jalapeño, onion, lemon juice, oil, and mustard.

Add the fresh herbs to the salsa, and season to taste with salt and pepper. Serve the pork with the salsa.

YIELD: **4** TO **6** SERVINGS OF MEAT AND **2** CUPS (**250** g) SALSA

For the pork tenderloin:

2 pounds (905 g) pork tenderloin

Kosher salt and freshly ground black pepper

2 teaspoons (5 g) ground cumin

2 teaspoons (4 g) ground coriander

1 teaspoon (3 g) ground mustard

For the salsa:

3 medium-ripe peaches, diced

12 cherry tomatoes, quartered

1 jalapeño chile, seeds and ribs removed for less heat, diced

1/4 medium-size sweet onion, diced

2 tablespoons (30 ml) lemon juice

3 tablespoons (90 ml) olive oil

2 teaspoons (8 g) Dijon mustard

1/4 cup (4 g) loosely packed fresh cilantro and mint leaves, coarsely chopped

If you're using a gas grill, heat one zone of the grill to high and one to low. If you're using a charcoal grill, move the coals to one side to make a two-zone fire.

◌ **Peaches with Moscato Syrup** ◌

When peaches are at their peak, it almost seems a shame to cook them. This simple dessert adds elegance to raw Southern summer peaches, accentuating rather than masking their flavor. Moscato is a sweet, fizzy wine from Northern Italy that goes great with them. This recipe makes more syrup than you'll probably need, but it's delicious drizzled over all kinds of desserts, from fruit, to ice cream, to cake.

2 cups (475 ml) Moscato wine

2 cups (400 g) granulated sugar

1 vanilla bean, split in half

4 or 5 medium-size peaches

1 tablespoon (15 ml) fresh lemon juice

Combine the Moscato, sugar, and vanilla bean in a medium-size saucepan, whisk to combine, and bring to a simmer over medium-high heat. Reduce the heat and simmer, uncovered, 30 to 45 minutes, or until the liquid has reduced by half. Remove and discard the vanilla bean.

Cut the peaches in half lengthwise working around the pits, twist to separate the halves, then pull or cut out the pits. Cut each half into quarters lengthwise. Combine the peach slices and lemon juice in a bowl, and toss to coat the peaches. Serve the peaches in a bowl drizzled with as much syrup as you'd like.

YIELD: **4** TO **6** SERVINGS

ᦟ **Coconut Peach Crumble** ᧠

A simple fruit crumble is the South's signature summer dessert. Coconut flakes give this crumble tropical flavor. Be sure the crumble topping is spread evenly to only about ¾-inch (2 cm) thick (reserve some of the topping if you need to) before baking, which will ensure the crust gets crispy.

Place the rack in the middle part of the oven, and preheat to 375°F (190°C, or gas mark 5).

Cut the peaches in half lengthwise working around the pits, twist to separate the halves, then pull or cut out the pits. Cut each peach into sixteen slices. Combine the peaches and lemon juice in a bowl and toss to combine.

In a medium-size bowl, whisk together ¼ cup of the brown sugar, the cornstarch, and lemon zest until combined. Sprinkle this mixture over the peaches, and gently toss to coat the peaches. Transfer the peaches to a 13 x 9 x 2-inch (33 x 23 x 5 cm), or similar size, shallow baking dish.

In a medium-size bowl, stir together the remaining ¼ cup brown sugar, oats, all-purpose flour, shredded sweetened coconut, cinnamon, and salt. Add the butter in pieces, and pinch everything together with your fingers until large crumbles form.

Spread the topping over the peaches to a depth of about ¾ inch (19 mm). Bake 30 to 40 minutes, or until the topping is golden brown and crispy and the filling is hot.

YIELD: **4** TO **6** SERVINGS

2 pounds (905 g) ripe peaches

¼ teaspoon fresh lemon juice

½ cup (110 g) light brown sugar, divided

1 tablespoon (8 g) cornstarch

1 teaspoon (2 g) freshly grated lemon zest

½ cup (40 g) rolled oats

½ cup (60 g) all-purpose flour

1 tablespoon (15 g) shredded, sweetened coconut

½ teaspoon ground cinnamon

Pinch kosher salt

8 tablespoons (¼ pound, or 57 g) unsalted butter, cut into pieces, at room temperature

WATERMELON

In the kitchen, I like to think of the watermelon as a sweeter version of the tomato. For example, watermelon dovetails with gazpacho, rounding out the acidity and adds new and interesting flavors to that timeless chilled soup from Spain.

Salty, crumbly cheeses, such as feta and ricotta salata, pair beautifully with watermelon's candy-like sweetness and crystalline texture. Mint, marjoram, and other bold, woodsy herbs offer a similar stark but pleasing contrast, as do pungent, savory aromatics, such as onions and fresh ginger.

I love to preserve watermelon's inherent flavor in a simple watermelon granita or make a chutney with the discarded rind. Watermelon simmered with vinegar and Indian-inspired spices is delicious alongside roasted meats. When grilled, watermelon takes on a whole new flavor, especially when paired with sweet shrimp and smoky eggplant.

The watermelon belongs to a group of seed-filled climbing vines in the same family as the cucumber, squash, and gourd. It likely first grew wild thousands of years ago in southern Africa, where it was eventually domesticated and became prized for its water-holding abilities in a dry climate. From there, it spread around the world. Signs of watermelon cultivation have been found as far back as 3,000 years ago in India, and in the Nile delta of Egypt. Like collards and field peas, watermelon is said to have made its way to the Americas and to the South via the slave trade from Africa.

Today's watermelon come in lots of varieties, from sugar baby to crimson sweet to yellow—there are even square varieties. There are more seedless watermelons now than ever, and I like to eat and cook with those, all things being equal, because they're easy to work with. But seedless or not, I lean toward unusual varieties. The most important predictor of taste and flavor, as with just about any produce, is how it was grown, whether it was harvested when ripe, and how long and how rough the trip was from farm to table.

Choose a watermelon that is free of blemishes and feels heavy for its size. Depending on how they're grown, many watermelons will have a normal "field patch," or flat discolored spot, where it rested on the ground when growing. Refrigerate uncut watermelon for an hour or two just before serving; chilling too long will degrade its flavor and texture. Unused portions of watermelon should be tightly wrapped or covered and used within a few days. And you can always purée any remaining sweet flesh, freeze it, and use it in these and other recipes.

❧ Steak Tacos with Watermelon Salsa ❧

If you're using a gas grill, heat one zone of the grill to high and one to low. If you're using a charcoal grill, move the coals to one side to make a two-zone fire. Rich, flavorful, tender skirt steak is a great match with this sweet and spicy watermelon salsa, topped with shaved raw cabbage for crunch, and salty, tangy Mexican cheese.

To prepare the steak: Season the steak on both sides with the salt and pepper, cinnamon, cumin, and coriander. Refrigerate for at least 1 hour and up to overnight. Bring to room temperature before grilling.

To make the salsa: Combine the jalapeño, watermelon, cilantro, onion, lime juice, and olive oil, and season to taste with salt and pepper. Add more lime juice, olive oil, or cilantro if desired.

To make the steak: Preheat the grill to high, brush the steaks on both sides with olive oil, and cook the steak to desired doneness, turning once, 4 to 6 minutes per side for medium-rare (130°F, or 54°C, when measured in the thickest part with a meat thermometer). Set the steak aside to rest, loosely covered with foil, for 10 minutes.

To make the tacos: Wrap the tortillas in aluminum foil and warm on the grill or in an oven on low heat until just steamy and pliable. To assemble the tacos, divide the steak, salsa, cheese, and cabbage among the tortillas, and top with the garnishes, as desired.

YIELD: 4 TO 6 SERVINGS

For the steak:

1 pound (455 g) skirt steak

1 teaspoon (6 g) kosher salt, or to taste

Freshly ground black pepper

¼ teaspoon ground cinnamon

¼ teaspoon ground cumin

¼ teaspoon ground coriander

Olive oil, as needed

For the watermelon salsa:

1 medium-size jalapeño, minced

½ small seedless watermelon, cut into ½-inch (13 mm) pieces (about 6 cups, or 900 g)

½ cup (8 g) minced fresh cilantro

⅔ cup (110 g) minced red onion (about ½ medium-size red onion)

4 tablespoons (60 ml) fresh lime juice

1 tablespoon (15 ml) extra-virgin olive oil

Salt and freshly ground black pepper

For the tacos:

Warm corn or flour tortillas

8 ounces (225 g) cotijo cheese, crumbled

4 cups (280 g) shredded green cabbage

Optional garnishes:

Diced avocado

Chopped fresh cilantro leaves

Sour cream

Freshly squeezed lime juice

Hot sauce

❧ Grilled Shrimp and Watermelon Kebabs with Lime Cream and Basil ❧

This is a Spanish-inspired unusual combination of flavors that work really well together, made Southern with fresh ingredients from my garden. Grilling eggplant brings out a smoky flavor, and the watermelon takes on an unexpected earthiness enhancing the sweetness of the shrimp. I like to serve these kebabs on a bed of red, black, or basmati rice.

To make the lime cream: Add the sour cream, lime juice, zest, and onion to a small bowl, stir to combine, and season to taste with salt and pepper.

To make the kebabs: Preheat the grill to high. Divide the shrimp, eggplant, and watermelon among 8 to 10 skewers, alternating the ingredients. Season each kebab generously with salt and pepper, paprika, cumin, and coriander. Brush each with olive oil.

Grill the kebabs over high heat until the shrimp is cooked through and the eggplant and watermelon are sweetened and charred, turning once, 4 to 6 minutes per side. Scatter the basil leaves over the kebabs, and serve with the lime cream.

YIELD: **4** TO **6** SERVINGS

For the lime cream:

1 cup (230 g) sour cream

½ cup (120 ml) freshly squeezed lime juice

Zest from 1 lime

1 scallion, green and light green part only, thinly sliced

Salt and freshly ground black pepper

For the kebabs:

2 pounds (905 g) medium-size shrimp, peeled and deveined if desired

2 small eggplant (about 1 pound, or 455 g each), cut into 1-inch (2.5 cm) pieces (about 4 cups, or 328 g)

½ small seedless watermelon, cubed (about 4 cups, or 600 g)

Kosher salt and freshly ground black pepper

1 teaspoon (2.5 g) sweet smoked paprika

½ teaspoon ground cumin

½ teaspoon ground coriander

Olive oil, as needed for brushing the skewers

6 to 8 fresh basil leaves, torn into pieces

⅋ Sicilian Watermelon Pudding ℰ

When I lived in Rome after college, I spent three weeks traveling through Sicily and came across this festive sweet pudding in Palermo. It has an almost candy-like quality that bespeaks Sicily's Arab influence, flecked with slightly bitter chocolate, crunchy pistachios, and chopped with pillowy whipped cream.

Purée the watermelon in a food processor until smooth. Whisk together the sugar and cornstarch in a medium-size saucepan, and whisk in the puréed watermelon. Add the mint leaves, sea salt, cayenne pepper, and almond extract, and bring the mixture to a boil over medium-high heat, stirring often. Reduce the heat and simmer, stirring constantly and scraping the bottom to prevent sticking, about 5 minutes, or until the mixture thickens. Remove from the heat and stir in the lemon juice; pass the mixture through a fine-mesh strainer placed over a large bowl. Pour the mixture into a medium-size casserole dish, and let cool. When cool, refrigerate, covered, for at least 4 hours or overnight. Serve with the garnishes, if desired.

YIELD: **6** TO **8** SERVINGS

2 pounds (905 g) seedless watermelon flesh, roughly cut into 1-inch (2.5 cm) pieces

²/₃ cup (133 g) granulated sugar

½ cup (65 g) cornstarch

6 to 8 fresh mint leaves, lightly bruised

Pinch sea salt

Pinch cayenne pepper

1 teaspoon (5 ml) almond extract

1 tablespoon (15 ml) lemon juice

Optional garnishes:

Chopped unsalted pistachios

Grated bittersweet chocolate

Whipped cream

Sicilian Watermelon Pudding, *gelo di mellone*, is a specialty of the capital, Palermo. It's a beautifully colored and festive dessert with an almost jello-like texture. Topped with crushed pistachios, and grated chocolate, and served with whipped cream, it's a dessert that exemplifies the Sicilian penchant for mingling sweet, sour, and bitter flavors.

❧ Watermelon, Tomato, and Ginger Salad ❧

Southeast-Asian cuisines transform fresh humble ingredients into surprisingly complex tastes, flavors, and textures. This variation on Burmese ginger salad, or *gin thoke*, is inspired by one I had on a trip to Singapore last year. The unusual combination of fruits, nuts, seeds, legumes, and aromatics issweet, salty, sour, pungent, and crunchy—all at the same time.

Combine the lentils and 4 cups (1 L) water in a medium saucepan. Bring to a boil, reduce to a simmer, and cook until the lentils are tender but not falling apart, about 10 to 15 minutes. Drain, and season lightly with salt and pepper.

Meanwhile, combine the peanuts and sesame seeds in a dry skillet over medium heat. Cook, stirring often, until the peanuts and sesame seeds toast and turn light brown, 4 to 6 minutes, then transfer to a plate to cool.

Combine the cabbage, watermelon, tomatoes, green onions, toasted peanuts, and sesame seeds in a large bowl.

Heat the peanut oil in a medium skillet over medium heat. Add the garlic, and cook, stirring often, until the garlic is lightly toasted, 2 to 4 minutes. Add the grated ginger and lime juice, cook 30 seconds, then transfer to a bowl to cool.

Pour the cooled garlic, ginger, and oil mixture over the salad. Add the fish sauce and olive oil, and toss to combine. Adjust the seasoning with more lime juice, fish sauce, or olive oil, to taste.

YIELD: **4** TO **6** SERVINGS

1 cup (192 g) green lentils, rinsed and picked over

Salt and white pepper, to taste

1 cup (144 g) unsalted peanuts

⅔ cup (75 g) sesame seeds

2 cups (140 g) shredded green cabbage

½ small seedless watermelon, cubed (about 4 cups [600 g])

2 small yellow tomatoes, chopped

3 green onions, dark and light green parts only, thinly sliced

2 tablespoons (30 ml) peanut oil

2 cloves garlic, thinly sliced

2 teaspoons (4 g) minced or grated fresh ginger

1 tablespoon (15 ml) lime juice, plus more to taste

3 tablespoons (54 g) fish sauce, plus more to taste

1 tablespoon (15 ml) extra-virgin olive oil, plus more to taste

❧ Watermelon Ginger Granita ❧

This simple granita is a great way to punctuate a summer meal. The ginger gives the granita a burst of spicy heat, and the acidity of the lime balances out the watermelon's sweetness.

⅓ cup (115 g) honey

1 teaspoon (2 g)minced or grated peeled fresh ginger

8 cups (1.2 kg) seedless watermelon chunks (about 2½ pounds)

2 tablespoons (30 ml) fresh lime juice

Combine the honey and ginger in a small saucepan and warm over low heat about 5 minutes, or until the honey softens and becomes infused with the ginger flavor.

Combine the honey and ginger mixture, watermelon, and lime juice in a food processor, and purée until smooth. Pass through a fine-mesh strainer into a large bowl. Refrigerate, covered, for 2 hours or overnight.

Pour the chilled mixture into a casserole dish and freeze, periodically scraping the mixture with a fork to loosen, about 4 hours, or until granita consistency.

YIELD: ABOUT 1 QUART (800 g)

A granita is a frozen dessert made with water, fruit purée, sugar and other flavorings, and varies in texture from chunky to smooth. Likely originating in Sicily, granita are simple to make with just a freezer and a fork, refreshing in hot climates, and easily adapted to accommodate a wide range of ingredients.

❦ COOKING NOTES ❦

PRODUCT QUALITY

Many of these recipes in this book are simple, and rely on the quality of the produce and herbs, meat and seafood, cheeses, eggs, grains, spices, and condiments you're cooking with. The better quality the products you have, the better tasting the food you cook. It's important to have (or learn) cooking techniques in the kitchen, but if the products you're using are subpar, the quality of the finished dish is limited from the outset.

With produce, the shorter the span of time between harvest and table, the better your food will taste. With meats, that time span and especially how those animals are fed and treated are important to their flavor. With seafood, freshness and handling, as in how cold it is kept, are key. There's just no way around this.

None of us can, for practical and economical reasons, always use the best-quality ingredients. Just know that quality has a big affect on the final product, especially with recipes meant to highlight those ingredients. For my part, I'd rather cut out meat two nights a week to be able to spend twice as much two other nights to use the meat from top-quality animals that were raised in the natural conditions they evolved to live in.

HERBS

Fresh herbs transform and elevate simple cooking. Buy them, grow them, have them on hand, and experiment with them. There simply is no substitute for the amount of interest and flavor they add, as with a flourish of parsley at the end of a dish or a sprig of thyme when roasting vegetables. Many of the recipes in this book rely on herbs for significant flavor. Omit them and the dish won't taste as good. Herbs are an easy way to cheat and make your simple everyday food stand out.

CITRUS AND VINEGAR

The next time you make a stew that simmers for half an hour or more on the stove, taste it, and then stir in a dash of vinegar or lemon juice, and taste it again. This brightening or waking up of the flavor makes a big difference in the final flavor of a dish. Buy different vinegars and citrus fruits and experiment. I use a lot of citrus zest, which has a lot of flavor by volume and gives many dishes great depth of flavor.

SALT AND SEASONING

Seasoning with salt is at the top of the list in terms of skills a cook can develop on his or her own to become a better cook. My hope is that if you think you really need measured amounts of salt when you cook, that you put that thought aside and start practicing now, without measuring. Most of these relatively simple recipes can be seasoned with salt as you go along. Unless it's an assembled and baked dish, there's no need to use a lot of salt up front. You can always add more but can't take it back.

I mostly use kosher salt because I like the feel of it in my hands and can tell how much I'm using. I also use a coarse sea salt, such as Maldon, usually at the end of cooking the simplest of dishes (like the first recipe in this book), in which you can actually taste the salt and appreciate its texture. Table salt is twice as salty by volume as kosher salt, and there's lots of variation in between, which is another reason I err on the side of not giving amounts. Pick a salt you like, season lightly at first, taste, reseason, taste, and reseason. You'll get better and better at judging how much salt to add.

PEPPER

I keep a good quality peppermill on hand filled with fresh black peppercorns and adjust the grind depending on the dish I'm cooking: finer when I want it to disappear or dissipate, such as in delicately flavored vegetable dishes, soups, and stews, and coarser when I want its flavor and texture to stand out, such as with steaks. I use white pepper where I want less color, with gratins, or want the pepper to fade into the background.

CHILE FLAKES, CAYENNE PEPPER, AND FRESH CHILES

I use all kinds of dried pepper flakes and fresh chiles in cooking. In general, the flavor and levels of heat are different from variety to variety and even from chile to chile within varieties. The heat in jalapeños, for example, varies a lot. There's no substitute for experience here either, so pick a few and experiment.

I use dried red pepper flakes almost as much as black pepper, as you'll see in many recipes, and often use cayenne pepper, too. I keep dried chiles from Japan and Korea on hand and love experimenting with different types. Dried chiles and pepper flakes are great to order online.

Fresh chile-wise, I can always find loads of red and green Thai chiles at my local Asian market, so I use those often. They're small, hotter, and easier to slice than most jalapeños and not as hot as most serranos, two more peppers I can usually find. I love habaneros for their fruity flavor and heat, but they're so hot I almost always cut out their seeds and ribs unless it's a really big dish. Remembering to wash your knife, cutting board, and, above all, hands after handling chiles, especially habaneros, is vital. Not doing so then touching your eyes, nose, or lips is usually something you only do once or twice.

STOCKS AND BROTHS

Chicken stock, vegetable stock, and fish broth are essential in classic French cooking. I don't often make them, but instead throw whatever I have on hand—a few chicken wings, onions, shallots, peppers, carrots, celery, ginger, a bundle of herbs, a chile or peppercorns—in a pot, cover with water, season generously with salt, and simmer for 30 minutes or so to make a flavorful liquid.

With most soups and stews, I find that water and the ingredients themselves often lend enough of their own unique flavor to make a dish taste really good. Sometimes chicken stock overpowers a dish. I like to make more subtle Japanese broths with dashi and kombu, and simple mushroom and vegetable broths with whatever I have on hand. Or I throw a bunch of shrimp shells or fish bones in water, simmer for 15 minutes, and use that broth in place of water with a fish soup or gumbo.

TOMATOES

Many of the recipes in this book call for some form of tomato, whether puréed; whole and peeled; peeled and seeded; and fresh, canned; or jarred. They all do pretty much the same thing, with varying degrees of freshness. When tomatoes are in season and plentiful, I'll purée the fresh ones for recipes that call for tomato purée, usually without seeding or peeling, neither of which bother me much. In the winter, I substitute jarred tomato purée or throw peeled fresh or canned whole or diced tomatoes in the food processor. Try different brands if using canned, and see which ones taste best to you.

MEAT DONENESS

There is nothing I can do in this cookbook to make sure your meat comes out perfectly cooked except to give you subtle tips and suggested temperatures. Knowing when the meat or fish reaches those temperatures either requires years of experience with poking meat with your finger as it cooks or buying a kitchen thermometer. Buy a kitchen thermometer. Meats vary in thickness, fat, and moisture content, all of which affect cooking time, as do ovens, stoves, and grills. Check the temperature of cooking meat early and often. Losing track of time probably ruins more cuts of meat than anything else.

SERVING SIZE

Most of the recipes in this book serve four to six people. Since many of them can be eaten either alone as a meal or with one other dish for a complete meal, I like to make my servings generous. So, "serves 4 to 6" usually means the dish serves four people with very good appetites or six less-hungry people where a sidelike portion is adequate.

SUBSTITUTION

Please do. Recipes are guides, snapshots of dishes I've cooked from just a few to dozens of times. Whatever looks best to you at the market will taste the best in the final dish. Look for ingredients with similar textures, sizes, and cooking times, and it's hard to go wrong.

❧ RESOURCES ❧

BOOKS

Arabesque, Claudia Roden; Alfred A. Knopf, Inc.

Essentials of Cooking, James Peterson; Artisan Books

Mangoes & Curry Leaves and *Hot Sour Salty Sweet: A Culinary Journey Through Southeast Asia*, Jeffrey Alford and Naomi Duguid; Artisan Books

Taste: A New Way to Cook, Sybil Kapoor; Octopus Publishing Group

The Art of Simple Food, Alice Waters; Clarkson Potter

Vegetables from Amaranth to Zucchini, Elizabeth Schneider; William Morrow

INGREDIENTS

Kalustyan's
Specialty foods
kalustyans.com
800-352-3451

Amigofoods.com
Latin foods
800-627-2544

Dayna's Market
Mediterranean foods
313-999-1980

Importfood.com
Thai and Asian ingredients
888-618-8424

La Quercia
Hand-crafted cured meats
laquercia.us
585-981-1625

Niman Ranch
High-quality meats
nimanranch.com

Anson Mills
Southern, heirloom, and other high-quality grains
ansonmills.com

Whole Foods Market
Organic, sustainable, and local foods
wholefoodsmarket.com

Growfood Carolina
Connecting growers to grocers and the community
growfoodcarolina.com

Charleston Farmers Markets
Voted one of the top ten in the U.S.; dedicated to the
advocacy of local farmers
charlestonfarmersmarket.com

Murphree's Market, Birmingham, Alabama
The best of local plants, foods, and artisan goods
murphreesmarket.com

Washington, DC Farmers' Markets
Non-profit organization building the
local, sustainable food movement
freshfarmmarkets.org

INFORMATION AND INSTRUCTION

Brys Stephens
brysstephens.com

Cookthink
cookthink.com

America's Test Kitchen
americastestkitchen.com

Saveur magazine
saveur.com

Epicurious
epicurious.com

EQUIPMENT

Cooking Equipment
cooking.com
800-663-8810

Oxo
oxo.com

Le Creuset
lecreuset.com

All Clad
all-clad.com

Weber
weber.com

❧ ABOUT THE AUTHOR ❧

Brys Stephens is a writer, cook, and photographer based in Charleston, South Carolina. He has written for *Bon Appetit*, *Garden and Gun*, *Charleston Magazine*, and is a former restaurant critic at the *Charleston City Paper*. In 2006, he founded the cooking website, Cookthink.

❧ ACKNOWLEDGMENTS ❧

Thanks especially to my mom, Laura Hearn, my dad, Elton Stephens, Jr., my brother, Hampton Stephens, and my sister Forrest Staton, for a lifetime of love, support, and fun.

Thanks to my longtime hometown friend, editor, and collaborator, Chip Brantley. Thanks to the team at Fair Winds Press: Jill Alexander, Heather Godin, Betsy Gammons, Katie Fawkes, and Becky Gissel.

Thanks also to an array of colleagues who have directly and indirectly influenced this book: Chris Hastings, Frank Stitt, James Peterson, Matt Lee, Ted Lee, Sara Clow, Andrew Knowlton, Stephanie Barna, Darcy Shankland, Ricky Hacker, Matt McIntosh, Carlye Dougherty, Brad Norton, Laurel Bruner, Marion Sullivan, Holly Herrick, Nathalie Dupree, Hank Holliday, Frank McMahon, Graham Dailey, Melissa Bigner, Will Schwalbe, Barbara Kafka, Michael Ruhlman, Peter Kaminsky, Mike Lata, Sean Brock, Ken Vedrinski, Craig Williams, Tom Shelton, Buff Ross, and Carolyn Vass, who made much of the pottery you see in the book.

❧ CONCLUSION ❧

Like any cook anywhere in the world, professional or not, my cooking is influenced by my experiences: childhood meals, travel, dining out, reading, the weather, cravings, health, and time spent practicing and learning in the kitchen.

I talk about all of these things in this book. But, I've always distilled those influences into a love of place, and attached place to the ingredients that grow and come from there. The things that represent the essence of a place drive my cooking when I'm there, and that is why this book is organized the way it is, with each chapter an ingredient.

Because each of these ingredients is at home in the South, I think of them all as quintessentially Southern. But, they are not exclusive to the South, of course. Most of them thrive across the globe, and while they may have a long history in the South, most have much longer histories in other places. So, while this is a book about Southern cuisine, it is inspired, directly and indirectly, by cuisines that have evolved for thousands of years in places such as Peru, Greece, India, and China.

I hope the book also shows that as a Southerner living in the South, I think of my cooking as just as Southern as fried chicken and biscuits. In fact, I don't know many people who regularly cook fried chicken and biscuits as part of their daily diet anymore.

Like a vernacular architecture, vernacular Southern cuisine continually evolves. To me, this book is representative of that evolution. I don't mean to claim that this is the only, the best, or the complete *New Southern Table*. Instead, it's a snapshot of my own exploration of Southern vernacular as I cook for family, friends, and myself. I hope that sharing these geographical, historical, and place-based recipes and photographs might inspire other home cooks—and maybe some restaurant chefs, as well—as we all contribute to the evolving Southern table.

INDEX